3 ACES

3 ACES

A winning proposition of your life

DEVESH VITHLANI

PARTRIDGE
A Penguin Random House Company

To order additional copies of this book, contact
Partridge India
000 800 10062 62
orders.india@partridgepublishing.com

www.partridgepublishing.com/india

CONTENTS

Preface

Humans are driven by emotions and it can be positive or negative, constructive or destructive, motivating or de-motivating, encouraging or challenging. We all know that our thoughts get transformed into our actions; which in turn becomes our habit. And friends, habit is nothing but the reflection of a personality.

We are surrounded by an atmosphere which is an amalgamation of positive and negative vibrations. The kind of vibration which we transmit in the universe becomes the source for the similar kind of vibrations to tempt. It requires the right attitude (wisdom and commitment) to resist the flow of negative energy, once it starts flowing in and more importantly, ceasing the flow to begin.

The contents of this book is all about dealing with emotions, which we encounter in day to day life and building the right attitude around it.

Life is game and there are certain rules of the game; adopting a right tactic within the jurisdiction of set rules, will give you an edge in winning your game.

Like in a game of three cards (Also called Poker), if you are playing with 3 Aces; you are going to be a sure shot winner. Similarly in life; if you are a master of 3 A's—Approach, Attitude and Attributes; winning will be your habit and sky is your limit. This book is partitioned in 3 parts—Approach, Attitude and Attributes and hence named—**3 Aces**.

<u>Attributes</u> are something inherent; each human being is born with some unique characteristics, which derive their destinies.

<u>Approach</u> is the action one takes to excel. It is a powerful and crucial element of our lives. Driving the strong attributes with wobbly approach might lead to a junction, called failure.

<u>Attitude</u> is how one looks at the things and situations. In same condition, some break the records while others break themselves. The mere difference is in attitude.

I would like to present you all here, a 3 points package of winning; which I learnt hard way while struggling through tough waves to hit the shore.

Introduction

This book is dedicated to all readers, who have aspiration of something to achieve in their lives. We all are born with a chunk of talents, which are the inherent characteristics of every individual. What most of us lack is, in the way it need to be utilized and the direction it need to be propelled.

When we look around, we find numerous faces with abundance of talents but scarcity of motivation and direction have put them on hold.

Daily and chaotic routine has occupied almost everything in our life that we are left with any span to look beyond it. High competition and limited availability has taken off the focus from need to stay in peace. Peace comes from wisdom. But where does wisdom come from? Wisdom comes from self realization. Now, some will think that this is one more piece of information on spiritualization. Self realization is knowing yourself in what you want, why you want that, how are you going to achieve it, what are the attributes you hold, what approach you need to espouse and the attitude you need to engulf.

In hard times, people have propensity to either retaliate or realize. What you look at, becomes your way of looking at life. Retaliation leads to frustration in your life as well as around you. Realization creates space for the self development and peace within & around you.

When, I was suffering through the hardest phase of my life during my teen age, I managed to learn from my own mistakes. It initially was painful to accept my own mistakes, but later I became at ease. I failed in relationships, career and financial ways.

I did Aircraft Maintenance Engineering and that too, with the help of scholarship; but could not get job. My father passed away when I was in higher schooling and my mother did all the hard work to get me there. I used to burst in tears alone. I even faced days, when every month, almost for half a month, I used to have only one meal a day, as I could not afford to take money from my mother anymore and my so called salary was too small to hold me for the entire month, after paying room rent and managing other expenses. I was in New Delhi those days in the year 2000. To save Rs 2 a day against a bus ticket, I had to take a walk for around 10 kms to reach my office. I used to save Rs 500 a month so that I can fund my further studies. My pockets were dead but aspirations had some more breaths; which kept me alive. I sometimes used to curse my life but I got to learn quickly that retaliation is not the key; it's just like sitting next to the locked door and weeping. The choice further was, continue doing Weeping and Creeping or find the key. Of course, I decided to embrace a hard path to stumble on a key. I made many mistakes on the way. Every day, numerous times, I used to remind myself of promise I made to myself; that was to realize and learn from every setback I face and will never look back. This was the hidden key in the treasure hunting game of life. I got to realize this when I reached to a level, which was far beyond my imagination that time.

Your potential of doing something does not always determine your destiny; your attitude has a bigger role to play.

Do not retaliate; make it a practice to realize. I promise you friends with the help of this book that this will change your life; as it changed mine.

ACE NO. 1
APPROACH

Self Talk

What is Self Talk? How it affects our personality? What are the benefits and challenges of Self talk? How to get most out of the self talk?

We indulge in communication activity in two different ways; one is with others and the other is with self, which is called Self Talk. Knowingly or unknowingly; intentionally or unintentionally, we get indulged in self communication almost every now and then, discussing various circumstances and feelings within. Self talk is a very common activity with every human being.

> We indulge in communication activity in two different ways; one is with others and the other is with self, which is called Self Talk.

The quality of self talk decides our reactions to a specific circumstance. Self talk engraves the path within the mind and we unconsciously starts following it. Self talk can be either positive or negative. The positive self talk forms energized and motivated path. On the other hand, a negative self conversation leads to a miserable path.

Whatever situation you encounter, you pose self opinion by means of self talk. So be fair and positive, when you suggest something to yourself. Don't throw good money for the bad; think only towards achieving something and don't be worry of losing something. During your journey to life, you certainly come across circumstances many times, which drain your energy and motivation. Sometimes, you feel like losing to the circumstances. You either have a choice here to surrender to it, which most of us do easily; or you may like to explore it to maintain the inner strength. The best way to explore such situation, affecting your motivation is by asking relevant questions to yourself. But bear in mind that your answers need to be unbiased and you need to be fair with your answers. Say for instance; if you are facing a threat of losing job, look at the **kind of questions you should ask to yourself**, so as to stop worrying and heading your thoughts in the right direction—

a) Does this job loss really a threat for me?
b) What can be the consequences, if this really happen to me?
c) Am I prepared to deal with these consequences?
d) What should I do to avoid or reduce the ill impact out of this situation?
e) If I keep worrying, is it going to help me?

f) Is this the end of the world for me?

g) What corrective action I need to take and by when?

h) What are the measures, I should take to avoid such circumstances in future?

You can challenge your negative thoughts with these kinds of questions for any threatening or worrying situation. No surprise, if you come out of it with light heart and relaxed mind.

> The outcome of the self talk depends on the way you initiate and chair the self talk.

With most of the cases, we simply transform and absorb worries out of self talk. Rarely, we try to dissect the situation this way. One should dissect the situation with intentions to—

1. Identify the problem or potential threat; is it really something to worry?

2. Judge the intensity of the threat; how big is the threat?

3. Gauge the impact it can have; what could be the ultimate impact?

4. Look for the possible solutions and people who can help you.

5. Look for the possibilities to avoid similar situations in future.

The outcome of the self talk depends on the way you initiate and chair the self talk. When you question your emotions and ask for the probable solutions within, you are actually helping yourself to step away from the negative influences.

Plan a different day

You go to shop to buy fashion material or home appliances; you look for variety to choose from. This gives you a satisfaction that you have gone through a wider scale of product range and what you selected is among the best. But do we really act the same way when it comes to our own way of living a life? We get boxed into the routine activities and that too, to an extent that we can't even think of breaking the ice.

> Discipline shapes life and Freedom colors it with liveliness.

There was a rich and very successful business man. At a very young age, he was awarded as one of the most talented young entrepreneurs in the world. When he was asked, what is the secret of his success; he replied Discipline! He was a very particular about driving the things as per his schedule and routine. He always believed in controlling time rather than he being controlled by time. So, he had schedules and routines fixed for most of his activities; he didn't like to compromise those at any cost. One of the attributes of successful people is that they are focused; they know what they are doing and why. So did this guy. He daily used to start his day early, at 5:30 am; exercising, reading news paper and getting ready for the office were the activities in his first 2 hours of day. He then used to spend 30 minutes in planning before he takes his first task of the day. He used to be in office by 9 am every day without fail until 7 pm. He never picked up any meetings or social activities post 7 pm. As per his schedule, one can always find him at home after 8pm. Like any other activity, he was particular about his dinner timing, which was 9 pm. Likewise; his bed time was clocked for 9:45 pm.

One day, he was taken to hospital from his office due to some sudden drop in health bar. He was only 35 years then and doctor declared that a life threatening disease found its way into his body, called Cancer. He was stunned. He had lot many goals and milestones to accomplish. He was under observation and treatment in the hospital for some time. During this period, he had enough time to look back and calculate the returns on his investments. In terms of wealth, he got the highest returns; however in terms of happiness, he was bare handed. He struggled within, to understand why he was having a feeling of emptiness when he owns the very best of things in the world. One day, while nursing, a nurse generally asked him," Sir, I am sure, you will be alright and get back to your normal life soon; and then what one thing will you do, which you have not done yet?" He was tongue tight to her question; but that made him think in a different way and he came up with one word answer to him; that was "Change". He never allowed any change in his life; he never tried to taste different flavors, he never believed in variety.

A couple of months later, he was declared free from his life threatening disease. But, those two months changed the way he was looking at life. This time he bounced back with an introduction of a character in his life, called variety. He had some routine lined up, but this time not more than what was required. He kept some free time to utilize it flexibly. Not just that, he decided to spare one full day in a month in a different way to taste different flavors of life; like, he will work from home that day or he will go to office in jeans and T-shirt once in a month; or he will organize a cricket match for his staff or spending a day with self without being interrupted by any calls or mails. He slowly felt liveliness in his life and started enjoying it.

That is what the strength of 'Variety' in our life. Adding spice of variety in our life, changes the taste and fragrance of it completely. I personally like this concept, "A different day in a month." You can designate a day in a month, where you will be doing one thing different than your routine and you can keep changing the activity every month; like,

1) Spending a day with family only
2) Connecting with old friends and relatives

3) One may even like to speak less for that day. I do it sometime. I restrict myself to speak anything until and unless very much required. This recollects the energy and energizes you; also it helps you to indulge in self talk, which provides you inner sight.

4) No phone calls and emails

5) Indulging in an activity of your hobby, like painting, writing an article or poem, photography, etc.

6) Getting involved in some social activity.

You can never imagine how this addition of varied flavors will help you to feel life differently. By this kind of free activities, you set your soul free. Discipline shapes life and Freedom colors it with liveliness. 'A different day' concept gives you an opportunity and platform to hold an award each in your hand—Life and Liveliness.

Path to a Vision

Vision is the flight of fantasy. You need to dare to board that flight. Leave all your worries and nagging doubts on the run way itself. Let you only carry the baggage of free thoughts, ideas and wishes. Tighten your soul with enthusiasm and go like a dream.

Vision is the flight of fantasy. You need to dare to board that flight. Leave all your worries and nagging doubts on the run way itself.

To succeed in your life, imagination is equally required as of knowledge. William Arthur Ward said that if you can imagine it, you can do it.

Hardly, few people are having clarity on the purpose of their lives; majorities find difficulty in exploring the same. They act as lame duck in their own life, which is helpless to sail against the wind. The direction of their own life is dependent completely on the external factors. They keep moving in life, rather than moving their lives.

Nobody has achieved anything in his life without first exploring the very purpose of his life. To explore that, we first need to have a vision; vision of reaching somewhere, vision of achieving some goals. In short, it is the flight of fancy. Let your thoughts flow freely; let it get settle for something which makes you feel proud, happy and satisfied.

Fortunately, some have vision for themselves. They are all set to excel and succeed but difficulties they deal with are, where to start and how to.

There are few basic steps to lead to a purposeful life, those are—

1. Spark a thought,
2. Convert that thought(s) into Dream,
3. Shape the dream to a Vision,
4. Prepare the action plans to transform vision into reality
5. Lastly and very importantly, Act on it.

It seems simple, but believe me, it is not. On the way are involved—difficulties, challenges, hurdle of various shapes & sizes, failures & at times frustration ready to take you over.

One who has a patience & right attitude to excel, along with the required skills, can only be able to convert thoughts into vision and finally to reality.

Excelling in path comes later; before comes difficulty in selecting a start point; from where should

I start. Enacting the starting point is more difficult and energy consuming than to shape an amorphous (shapeless) finishing line.

Initial cranking of an engine consumes higher fuel & energy as compared to the state, where an engine is running at an optimum speed and capacity. The same way, sparking a thought and shaping it into the vision is an impetus job. It may be required to rework again and again on defining a starting point, before heading at the convergence of Dream & Reality.

> Before they became hero of other's life, they first became hero of their own lives.

Karoly Takacs, was a right handed pistol shooter, from Hungary. He was in the Hungarian Army and was known for his sharp shooting skills. He wanted to participate in the Olympics but he being in the sergeant rank, was not allowed to compete, as the participation was limited to only commissioned officers that time. But later this ban was removed. He was now gunning at 1940 Olympics, which was to be held in Tokyo.

In 1938, due to a faulty grenade explosion, his right hand got badly injured. He was then left with only one hand, which was not his core hand. He was right handed shooter and now he had to start again from the scratch in training his left hand. After bouncing back from this set back, he secretly started practicing. Surprisingly, in 1939, he bagged the national shooting championship. He was now all set for 1940 Olympics. But because of Second World War, Olympics games scheduled for 1940 and 1944 were got cancelled. He now had to wait for another 8 yrs to compete in Olympics; which he did. He surprised the world by winning the gold medal in 25 meter rapid fire pistol event in 1948 Olympics in London with his only hand. He again repeated the history by winning another gold medal in next Olympics in 1952 in Helsinki.

Let's study this true story in relation with what is mentioned above.

1. Karoly had a spark within to compete in Olympics.
2. He persuaded with his thought of competing in Olympics and he was dreaming of his performance in Olympics.
3. He committed himself to transform his dream into reality. He created that vision in his mind and was working life and death to make it true.
4. He planned and trained himself for Olympics games to come; he worked hard in practicing with his only hand.
5. Where everyone was competing with their best hands, he was competing with his only hand. Didn't matter to him; his focus was on delivering the best with what was left with him—The only hand.

6. After setting vision and even working hard towards it, difficulties did come in his life. But his focus was not on difficulties and hurdles. Temporary setbacks like cancelling of Olympics twice, when he was fully prepared, didn't even shake his vision. On top of that the permanent loss of his core hand had no impact on his will to transform vision into reality. He did it.

There you find numerous such inspirations across the world. You go and check out their success stories; you will find the same journey, which they covered in their lives.

Thought———→ Dream————→ Vision————→ Planning————→ Action

With the adoption of this path, people like Karoly, have become hero of other's life. But before they became hero of other's life, they first became hero of their own lives.

Creating Dreams

Imagine, if cricket is to be played without tracking and tracing scores; Teams have to be played without competing and chasing the numbers; no goal nets were to be seen at either end of the ground and football to be played without scoring goals. How does this sound? Interesting or boring?

> It is the purpose to chase the numbers and purpose to win; that makes the game exciting.

There is a purpose involved in each game. It is the purpose to chase the numbers and purpose to win; that makes the game exciting. Be it a game or a life. What sets the purpose? The Dream! Dream to conquer, Dream to feel the sense of achievement.

It is imperative to first create a dream for yourself; this will give you a purpose in your life. Once you have the purpose, associate the same with some tracking numbers, like—

1. In how many years/months, you would like to reach to your destiny;
2. How much money you want to save and by when; etc

Once, you associate numbers with your goals, like above; journey to destiny becomes fun filled. You start enjoying journey and that is the key to success. When we enjoy journey more than the goal itself, it gives a real pleasure. Once you set your dreams and start working towards it, your energy level automatically gets boosted and thought levels started flowing to positive side of the world. Suddenly, you start looking at the world altogether from a different angle.

Most of the people don't realise the importance of having a definite purpose; they end up sailing with time without having control over it. They choose a boring path rather than an exciting & interesting track to play a game of life. It's altogether your own choice, what kind of game you choose to play; One without any goals or one with fun, challenges & excitement.

Get set your dreams right now; you will be amazed with the excitement of chasing the definite purpose and goals. A day, when you happen to make

> When we enjoy journey more than the goal itself, it gives a real pleasure. .

your dream come true; the feeling, you encounter there, would be out of the world, believe me.

Don't let your boat sailed by waves of time; let **YOU** have a control over the direction.

Setting Goals

Our life is not all beer and skittles; it has a definite purpose to deal. What would be life without goals? Certainly, directionless! When,

> When, we don't have a direction in our life, chances of devil attacks like depression, frustration etc will be high.

we don't have a direction in our life, chances of devil attacks like depression, frustration etc will be high.

You must know where you are heading and WHY. Goals and Plans are like road maps; they won't guarantee you a smooth journey but certainly gives you the directions. By setting goals, you define the purpose to your life. To set a goal, you need to have a Skill and Will. **Skill** of setting SMART goals, which we all know is a goal, which should be Specific, Measurable, Achievable, Realistic and of time bound and **Will** to achieve that goal. In order to bag it, you might have to work your finger to the bone. Once you are booked with your aim, don't look it with beady eye. Keep your aim on the goal and focus on the process. Most of the time, most of the people, focus on the goal and not on the process. They keep thinking about the result. You do not have to think about the output, not even once. When you know what is behind setting this goal (WHY?), it is enough and then pour every drop of your energy in the process to achieve it (HOW?). No matter, how far your destiny is but with the best will in the world, you can reach there.

You have two options; choose to survive or choose to succeed. If you let your boat sail directionless, you choose to survive and if you take a control of your boat, you choose to succeed. It is well said that where focus goes, energy flows. When you know what you want and why, your energy takes the charge and demonstrates how to achieve it.

Life works in strange ways. If you are focused and energized, the stranger will not be able to divert your attention. What are these strangers? These are frustration, failures, fear, criticism etc.

To understand the significance of goal setting, let's evaluate a simple paradigm. Suppose, the task is to travel from a place "X" to a destiny "Y"; there are four factors to be considered and evaluated—

Direction—to be headed, so as to reach "Y"
Distance—from where you are to your destiny
Speed—at which to travel; and

<u>Time</u>—required to cover the distance at a desired speed.

When I graduated, I was almost directionless; albeit I did Engineering thinking that I will get good job; and that was it in my mind when I pursued graduation. But that was certainly, not a goal; taking a good job was more of a requirement. It then took couple of years post that to recognize what I want from my life. Here I went and got bit of direction, I wanted to get into the senior management role in the blue chip company. Next step was to judge the distance. My soul was all set to fly as high as feasible to cover the gap from no one to someone. I studied on the academic and skill sets requirements for that position. Third challenge was to evaluate the speed at which I had to transport. I had to work to support my bread and butter, so giving the entire piece of the cake to the development activities was not feasible for me. But I planned and started working onto it parallel to my bread earning job. I enrolled myself for a distance learning education in management. On the other hand, I worked towards learning exponentially to sharpen the skills required for the desired position. It was now turn to estimate the time to reach to the goal. It then worked out to be 8-10 yrs. I could say that whatever I am today, it is because of that direction I set in 2002.

> Direction, Distance, Speed and Time are the key factors to a successful planning of professional and personal goals.

Now, let's look this from the scientific perspective; we all know the scientific relationship between Speed and Time. It is inversely proportional to each other; keeping distance a constant. This means that higher the speed, lesser would be the time required to cover a specific distance and vice-a-versa.

The very first requirement is to identify the "direction". If we have the direction but do not have a clue on the distance to be covered; can we work out on the speed requirement? Certainly NOT! Since speed and time are relative to each other; therefore, we can't define the time required to reach there. And that's the concern with most of us. First, we don't know where we want to be. Second, if we have some zeal to reach somewhere, then probably, most of the time having no idea on the direction, thereby misses other three crucial factors—Distance, Speed and Time.

In the absence of proper information on either of the above variables—Direction, Speed, Time and Distance, you will never be able to eat your piece of cake.

It is therefore very crucial to understand that Direction, Distance, Speed and Time are the key factors to a successful planning of professional and personal goals.

A thoughtful plan increases the probability of success, when drove with the right actions. This will avoid dooming yourself to failure.

Understanding, evaluating and considering the above 4 factors as ingredients in setting the goal, helps you to develop the required skill sets and importantly, creates a barrier for demon like frustration to impact you.

Success and Setting Goals

Success! I am sure majority of the world population is fascinated by this splendid word.

What is success? Different people have different way to define Success for them. But the key is to define it. Lot of people across the world does not even have a statement of success described for them.

I would emphasis on the below two concerns in this article—

- 1) Define Success
- 2) How do you achieve it?

<u>Defining success is the first step in achieving it</u>.

I would like to share an outcome of the survey, which was conducted by "Personal Selling Power"—A

Sales and Marketing Newsletter. The objective of the survey was to understand the meaning of success to different people and the responses were grouped into 3 different categories.

The 1st category was MATERIAL POSSESSION, which means—Position, Power, Bank Balance, Property etc.

The 2nd Category was EMOTIONAL Responses, where comes—Happiness, Family, Relationship etc.

The 3rd Category was PROCESS, where respondents believed in excelling from one destination to other like in Business, achieving various goals and consistent growth.

Material Possession after covering certain run ceases to satisfy you. Emotions are nebulous and dynamic. So the people from the first two categories are more prone to face serious consequences at any stage of their lives; whereas, the people from 3rd category have deeper foundation.

Now, how do you achieve success? There is no rocket science involved in it. A simple response from me to this is BY SETTING & GETTING GOAL. People who do not have a specific goals set with them are less likely to be more successful and more likely to earn less. To support this, I would like to share an another research conducted in Harvard University in the year 1979 and then again 10 years later in 1989. The objective was to understand the impact of setting goals.

MBA students were asked if they have written the specific goals with clear action plan for their future. Let's look at the responses below received in the research—

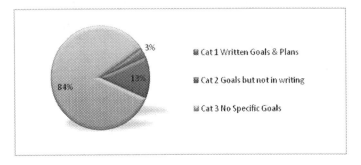

1. *Only 3% had specific goals and clear plans written with them.*
2. *13% had goals but not in writing*
3. *84% had no specific goals at all*

10 years later, in 1989, the same students were contacted back to check their career status. Here is the interesting figure—

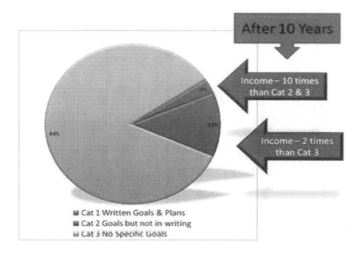

After 10 Years

Income – 10 times than Cat 2 & 3

Income – 2 times than Cat 3

■ Cat 1 Written Goals & Plans
■ Cat 2 Goals but not in writing
■ Cat 3 No Specific Goals

Students from category 2, who had some goals in mind but had no specific plans with it, were earning twice than that of category 3, who had no goals at all. Interestingly, students from category 1, who had specific goals with clear action plans were earning 10 times higher than the other both categories' students put together.

Goals are like Road Maps; they do not guarantee you a smooth journey but gives you the right direction, as to where to head on.

Many of us are scared to set goals. We fear of being disappointed on failing to achieve it. Most people believe that it would be better to have no goals and be pleasantly surprised when good things happen. It is interesting but a dangerous approach.

So far, two concerns were addressed. To recall, those were—

1) What is Success and
2) How to achieve it?

I am sure the next question popping up in the mind would be; how to set Goals?

Let's have a look below on the steps in setting goals. It consists of 7 steps—

1) What—First understand, what do you want to achieve/
2) Why—Why do you want to achieve it? If you know the reason, you would be able to stay motivated during the journey and not get easily frustrated.
3) When—By when do you want to achieve the goal? Set a timeline for your goal.
4) Information / support—List down the information and support, you may require to reach to your goal
5) People—Pen down the list of the people or the group, who might help you.
6) Action Plan—Very crucial. Frame the clear action plans.
7) Review—Lastly, don't forget to review your goals at regular interval, to ensure you stay on track.

We all are blessed with two lives; one, which we got and the other which we choose for ourselves. What kind of life we live depends on what kind of goals we set OR do not set at all.

At last, I would like to ask you, how would you like to see the last chapter of your life? Think about it and set your goals accordingly, NOW.

10 Things on setting and getting goals—

1. <u>Identify Needs</u>—The prime ingredient required in setting a goal; identifying the specific needs, albeit the needs may be more than one; but then the priority has to be set.

2. <u>Requirements to fulfil needs</u>—Once the need is identified, then it is mandatory to understand clearly, as to what are the requirements to accomplish those needs.

3. <u>Sources</u>—Third element of the process emphasis on the identification of the sources, which can help delivering the materials to achieve the end results.

4. <u>Set Goal</u>—Next step is to set a specific goal, like what to achieve and by when.

5. <u>Plan</u>—It's time to "Plot a Plan" on how to achieve the goal.

6. <u>Execution</u>—You are now ready with all the tools and the direction to head on towards the goal set, So give your plan a momentum.

7. <u>Track / Monitor</u>—Track the process and progress; co-relate the same with your expectations and norms.

8. <u>Relax a bit</u>—You have done what the best you can did so far, right from identification, execution to tracking. Allow yourself to relax a bit, while the output starts popping up in some time.

9. <u>Review</u>—Review the output. Is that what you expected? Is that the one which fulfil your need? If yes, then go to the next step; if not then you might like to jump to step no 2 and give a try again.

10. <u>Enjoy and Celebrate</u>—Congratulate yourself for the task done.

What, Why, Where & When!

I stepped out of an airport from Dubai; hired a taxi, dumped my luggage in the trunk and sat next to the driver's seat and said, "Let's go." He starred me with poker face. I then realized that I haven't told him "Where". I then laughed at myself inside that How weird was I!

Unfortunately, we treat our lives the same way, weirdly. We do not define WHERE we want to go.

Unfortunately, we treat our lives the same way, weirdly. We do not define WHERE we want to go; we simply sail with the waves and tell ourselves, let's go.

Once, a businessman was heading for a business conference. The conference was organized in one of the luxury resorts situated in the valley of the mountain; surrounded by lush green and breathe holding landscapes. He therefore

44

decided to go by road to enjoy the beauty of nature. He was astonished to witness on the way, the heart soothing greeneries and sensed the purity in air. No noise pollution, No chaotic phone calls and meetings, Nature's fresh flow of air with the fragrance far better and soothing than AC's blow; these different sensations encouraged him to feel nature more closely, so he decided to spend some time there and he stopped at one of the eye catching spots. It was around two o' clock in the noon but nature's fresh air didn't make him feel the need of Air Condition at all.

A little far, he noticed one small shop made of some wooden bars and tin sheets; the man was selling fresh fruits to the passers. He walked towards him and noticed that he was winding up his so called shop and was all set to head back to his home. The businessman was surprised and could not resist himself to ask him the reason for leaving for home so early, when he can sell some more fruits to the passengers and make more money for him and his family. The business man also asked him, "If you only work for half day; then what you do rest of the day?" To this the poor man replied that he gets up bit late at 8 am, spends some time at home, looks after his small farm, plucks some fresh fruits from trees; he then opens his shop at 9 am. He works until 2pm and then after lunch, he sleeps for an hour. He then plays with his kids and spends some time with his wife, takes a walk in the village in evening to see friends; extends help to his neighbours and fellow citizens, takes some part in village development activities and then finally goes to bed at 10 pm after dinner.

The businessman then tried to explain him what he is missing. He advised to the poor business man, "You should work until late in the evening; with this you can sell more and generate more money. With more money, you can invest in your business and in turn, you can make more profits. Again with more profits, you can hire someone to look after your shop and you can then open another shop in some other location. This will again help you to accumulate more wealth. With higher operating income, you can expand your business and can invest in purchasing more land to grow more fruits and then you can also start looking to export your fruits. With this you can even open your own company and shift to some big city from small village. This will give a better life style to your family. More wealth will eventually lead to power and status in the society." The poor chap thought for a while and innocently asked him," How much time will it take to reach to this level?" The businessman based on his wisdom and experience said, "Could be around 10-15 years." He then again asked the businessman," Once, I reach to that level then what?" The businessman was surprised to his question and offered him another suggestion," After that you can even open your branches in other countries and can generate more business." The poor man again asked the same question," Then what?" The businessman said," Then you can keep accumulating wealth and then get retire after 10 years; you can then have no worries on financial security for yourself and your family; this financial freedom will help you to enjoy full heartedly with your family, you can also join some recreation club to spend time with your friends or you can also do some charity to help needy or contribute in some form to society; this way you can gain more respect in family, friends and society." The poor man replied," don't you think that is what I am doing now?"

The poor business man had a clear understanding of WHERE he is and where he wants to be in his life, WHAT are his aspirations / strengths in life, WHY he wants that. No question on WHEN, as he was already dealing with what he wanted. The rich business man may have the clarity on what he wanted but may not justify why. He may have abundance of aspirations to set a plan by when he will be achieving, what are his aspirations and strengths, but may need some more thoughts to explore where he will end up.

One of the positive aspects of our life is to have wisdom of 4 W's in our life. We already know by now, which are these? We are here in this beautiful world for some definite purpose to fulfil. Sadly, majority of us are not well aware of the purpose of our lives.

If we throw 4 simple questions, especially to new generations; I am sure most of them would be speechless; and those are—

1. WHERE you want to reach in your life?
2. WHY you want to reach there?
3. WHEN you want to be there?

4. WHAT are your strengths, which will guide you there?

Most of us do not have the answers to these, and we therefore allow ourselves to sail directionless with time; thinking that one fine day we will reach somewhere!

How in this competitive world we are going to position ourselves, where we meant to, when we do not have the direction? It is therefore very crucial to explore the answers to the above questions to ascertain the purposeful life.

Mastering Time

D o you play the giddy goat, when you are loaded with the work and are not having enough bites in the hand?

Can we control time? What can we do if we are running short of time and have too many things to finish? Can we pause time, till we finish the intended work? What should we do when certain important things have been missed out and the deadlines have been crossed? Can we reverse the time to ensure nothing misses the deadline?

Certainly NOT! That means, we don't have control over time. But . . . . we can MASTER it. How?

By organizing our activities and setting priorities. This can be done by-

1. Preparing a master list of the tasks;
2. Assigning priorities to those tasks;
3. Estimating the completion time;

4. Assigning start time, and;
5. Assigning the completion time.

Prepare the master list of the tasks wished to accomplish. Depending on the workload, the size of the list may vary from few to real exhaustive one. However, the key here is to monitor the length of the list. If it seems too bulky, it is good to say no to new projects; until some space has been created by finishing some of the tasks. Else, it might result in chaotic and undue mental and physical stress. Placing tasks on the map, will give an overview on the overall length of time required to tick the box.

Mostly, those are the least important tasks which scream a lot & eat most of the time. Contrary, the most important tasks go silently. It is therefore mandatory to hammer out the scheme. This can be done by assigning priority codes U-Urgent, G—General, I—Important etc. Colour codes may also be used in conjunction with priority codes. This will help to put focus on important tasks first, before unimportant things take away most of the precious time.

It is crucial to know as to when a particular work is needed to be completed; that is, the deadline of the job; so that you can pay on the nail, else you will end up fighting tooth and nail at last minute to meet the deadline. Therefore, it is imperative to know how much time a project will take to finish. Once, you know both of these parameters, you can decide on assigning the start time to ensure it finishes on schedule time.

A sample tabular organizer is shown below for reference—

Sr.No	Job Description	Priority Code	Projected Time		Actual Time		Remarks / Comments for delay
			Start	End	Start	End	
1	Writing business plan	U	10.08.12	15.08.12	12.08.12	16.08.12	Delayed in collecting relevant stuffs

Necessity knows no laws. It is high time to pen down your own bylaws and manage the inflow-outflow in your favour. By managing your activities, you can keep your schedule within the letter of the law.

<u>True, we can't control time, but the good news is that we can Master it!</u>

Mind Management

I would like to reiterate that we all are blessed with 2 lives; one which we got and the other, which we choose for ourselves and that depends on

> We all are blessed with 2 lives; one which we got and the other, which we choose for ourselves.

how we manage our mind on the course of living and that is what called, Mind Management.

What are the various elements that influences human mind? These are—

1. Positive thinking—Most of the people bags misleading opinion about positive thinking. They believe that the person who walks with positive thinking; carries a smile always on his face; they are self energized, self motivated and are less likely to get affected by the negative influences. However, in reality, it embraces a different

message. Positive thinking is all about acting rather than reacting and there are 4 modes of transcendent to it, to explain it in a better way—

A) Self—Accept self; I do like myself. I am aware of my strengths and weaknesses. I believe in myself.

B) Others—Accept others the way they are. Believe in others, trusting and respecting them. Look for good in others.

C) Situation—Accept the reality of the situation, working with it rather than against it; believing that there is always a brighter side to it. Believing that whatever situation, I come across; has some positive purpose for me.

D) Goal—I am living for a definite purpose. Whatever situation and people, I come in contact with during my journey of life, good or challenging, will take me closer to my goal.

2. Anger / Frustration—Many of us find difficult to withdraw ourselves from the situation of anger/ frustration, once we are booked with it. There is a 3 step process involved with it in order to adieu it permanently—

A) Acceptance—Noticing yourself trapped in anger/ frustration, the immediate reaction to it is that you either try to suppress it or struggle with it. Don't do that. Suppressing will not help you for a long; it will bounce back again in some other form and at some other time. So accept it!

B) Observe—When you start observing your frustration or anger; you actually allow the disconnection of your emotions from the situation. The isolation of emotions then hands over the charge to your conscious mind. By acting as an observer, you stepped back from the circle of negative influence and withdraw energy from it. In the absence of energy (which is undue focus), the frustration or anger gets killed.

> Freedom is one thing that we all desire and deserve. Still why we ourselves cage our soul and act as a victim?

C) Return journey to peace—What happens when you bring an iron close to a magnet? It gets attracted towards it—Simple. Alright, will you be able to take it away from a magnet without applying any force? Certainly not. Till the time, the magnetism is there, it will try to hold an iron in place or else you have to apply the force higher than magnetism to withdraw the bar. But if you remove the magnetism itself, the isolation of iron bar with magnet can be done without effort. Similarly, once you took yourself out from the circle of negative influence (magnetism), it then becomes easy for you to head back to the inner peace. The best way is to meditate at least for 10-15 minutes in a day, especially at the end of the day. This helps you to wipe off the negative ashes in the mind and creates space for the positive thoughts to settle down and then you can start the next day afresh.

The more we focus on the situation that generates anger within, the higher the bar is raised. Imagine Anger as a tree and Focus as a water; what happens to a tree when you withdraw source of water from it? It decomposes and dies; that's what exactly we do, we withdraw focus and energy from a situation and your enemy will die at its own.

3. Free Soul—Freedom is one thing that we all desire and deserve. Still why we ourselves cage our soul and act as a victim? Since our childhood, we learn to live in a legitimate way; by following an inevitable path; no matters we love it or not. Most of us, while doing certain things, thinks this way that "I HAVE TO do this" rather than "I WANT TO do this"? When we say "I have to", we certify ourselves as a victim and act as a prisoner. This way we drag the life, rather than exulting it. Don't engulf your soul, set it free. Transform your action from "I HAVE TO" to "I WANT TO". This

transformation will dwell happiness in your soul and set peace within.

4. Self Awareness—The most crucial thing in managing self is self awareness. The first step in managing is awareness. If you are not aware of the fact, what will you manage? The first in mind management is self awareness; meaning awareness of your strengths and weaknesses. In a piece of paper, jot down both. You can take the help of your friends, relatives or mentors to explore it. Knowing and using your strengths, works as a tool to carve your path. On the other hand, the objective of identifying weakness is to shrug it off. How? By consciously working on it one by one. For instance, I listed few of my weaknesses and then picked up two, to start working on it. I used to take extra doses of sleep (8-9 hrs) and wanted to reduce to 7 hrs. To track it, I made 2 columns on one of the page of my diary; left to note dates and on right column to mention the hrs I slept that particular day. This way, I started monitoring it. I genuinely followed this for slightly more than a month (except weekends ☺). Believe me, it worked and post that I need not have to look back. The other factor which I wanted to shun was procrastination. Whenever, I felt like procrastinating something, I pressurized myself to get it done immediately. I did not go soft

with myself on this. Again after practicing it for few days, I got rid from it.

5. Negative Influencers—like ego, criticizing habit, impatience etc. have an ill effect in our life style. Almost everything in the world has the rudimentary principle applied to it and that is; there is a reaction to every action. So to shun these ill influencers, I suggest the same practice as illustrated above to shrug off the weaknesses.

6. Live in present; do not carry the burden of past on your head and don't dwell too much around future. Live in Present.

Someone said, "Difficulties do come in our life, to overcome it, you need to be strong and the strength comes only from the spiritual knowledge." And friends, this Spiritual knowledge is nothing but the Mind Management.

Timing Your Activities

It's a very known fact that Time flashes faster than the speed of anything in this world. We all are born with one common thing in hand, i.e;

> Its quiet shocking to understand that schedule for 75% of our time is almost fixed for specific tasks.

TIME. Difference is in one's approach towards handling it. Some deal with it very cautiously and others casually.

Your attitude towards this precious thing decides not only just your path but a destiny. We all have fixed 1440 minutes in a day, 525,600 minutes in a year. How we invest this asset and get the best out of the game, lies solely on the wise utilisation of it.

Many researches revealed that willingly or unwillingly, most of time is been wasted in unproductive activities or letting it pass without doing anything. Another concern is the over-investment of time; means, taking more than the required time in doing certain tasks, which is the absolute drainage of the fixed resource. Would anybody like to deal the same way when trading with money? Would you love to spend $1000, when the same thing you can get at $500. Many a times, we bargain so much while trading something with an intention to save few dollars. But do we really bargain with ourselves to save few minutes from every hour, by not wasting it?

Let's understand the statistics of time chart, as to what percentage of time is being used in various routine activities. We have fixed 24 hrs in a day. A typical daily activities and time expenditure thereof, under various activities are as below—

Sr. no	Activity	Avg time spend	% of total Time
1	Sleep	7 hrs	29%
2	Recreational activities- watching TV, reading Newspaper, talking to friends, with family, playing,etc.)	3 hrs	12.50%
3	Unaccounted activity	2 hrs	8.50%
4	Rest / Ideal period	2 hrs	8.50%
5	Freshning up (Brushing teeth, Bath, shaving, using toilets, putting up clothes etc.)	1 hrs	4.00%
6	Driving / Travelling	2 hrs	8.50%
7	Eating (all meals,BF, Supper)	1 hr	4.00%
		18 hrs	75%

Its quiet shocking to understand that schedule for 75% of our time is almost fixed for specific tasks. You are left with only 25% to test your calibre. How you play with this 25%, differentiates your path. A wise, careful and cautious utilization of this portion of time (or possibly the entire basket) gave birth to leaders like Dhiru bhai Ambani, Ratan Tata, Ajimji Premji, Aamir Khan, Muhammad Ali and so on. You name any successful personality in the world; they are successful not just because of the talent they have; but also the capability they possess in wisely using the time.

We are surrounded by so many time killers these days, especially in this e-era. E-gadgets, internet, social sites, mobiles, electronic games etc. If you carefully observe, you will surprise to understand that these are the real time-killers. They are meant for some utilization, but most of us, most of the time under utilize it and spend excess time on it.

Key here is to list down all the time-killers in a piece of paper, convince yourself to act over it, start cutting those one by one. Start working on one or two of it for a week and then gradually cover the rest. It will not call for any extra effort to make you feel, what you can buy with these hard saved precious time.

"Every second is of infinite value"—**Johann Wolfgang von Goethe**

"Don't say you don't have enough time. You have exactly the same number of hours per day that were given to Helen Keller, Pasteur, Michaelangelo, Mother

Teresea, Leonardo da Vinci, Thomas Jefferson, and Albert Einstein."—**H. Jackson Brown, Jr.**

"Time is what we want most, but what we use worst."—**William Penn**

"Time flies. It's up to you to be the navigator."
—**Robert Orben**

"Whether it's the best of times or the worst of times, it's the only time we've got, Use it wisely."—**Art Buchwald**

How to overcome your weaknesses

*T*his *is a story of 16yrs old boy and his grandfather. One day, the boy was upset, sitting all alone on the bench of a lawn beside his house. His grandfather noticed him from a window of his room. An hour passed and boy was still in the same posture—Worrying &*

> Weaknesses will be with you until you hold it; the moment, you decided to leave it, you will be free from it

Thinking. Grandfather thought that it's now time to see him; so he went to him, sat with him and asked if everything is alright. The boy swirled his head gently from left to right. His facial expressions were bleak.

Grandfather could make out that he is sailing through ordeal. He proceeded to dig child's heart gently and offered him a platform to share his worry. The child remained quiet for few seconds and then apprised his grandfather of his worry. He told him that he finds difficulty in catching up with either of Science subjects; he can't handle these perplexed subjects, which is a part of his curriculum. He had to face shameful appearance in the class most of the time; his amigos use to laugh at him and tagged him as duffer and that seethes him. He affirmed that he tried to overcome his weakness of coping up with the subjects numerous times but he didn't succeed.

His grandfather piffled at him that he has the secret of overcoming this weakness. He looked at his grandfather with bug-eyed. Grandfather invited him to see him at 6 am next day at the dining hall, if he wanted to explore that secret. That filled the child with some sanity and he accepted his grandfather's proposal.

Next day, as per the agreed schedule, the child entered the dining hall but could not see his grandfather. A little later, he could listen to his grandfather, yelling gently for help. He ran towards the direction of sound. He was astonished to see that his grandfather himself was embracing a pillar beneath the stairs and shouting for help to get relieved from it. With due respect, he asked his grandfather, why are you shouting for help when you, yourself can leave it in a second? His grandfather smiled at him; leaving his position, he started stepping towards his grandson and said that he got the lesson. Grandson exclaimed, "Which lesson?" The lesson of overcoming your own weaknesses, grandfather replied. He again exclaimed; "How come?" Grandfather then offered him a seat and elaborated that weaknesses will be with you until you hold it; the moment, you decided to leave it, you will be free from it and your enemy will disappear.

His grandfather's farce taught him the precious lesson that if you want to overcome your weaknesses, just decide to leave it and get rid of it. He was now into an inner exhilarating trip, which boosted his aplomb. Once you realize your power and rights, there you found in nascent stage of self actualization.

Thinking of weakness itself is panic. Who would like to see this corner of the story? Hardly

> God has sent us with raw mind and soul. We explore the world in different ways based on how we think and what we practice in our lives.

anyone; God has sent us with raw mind and soul. We explore the world in different ways based on how we think and what we practice in our lives. No one has been packaged as perfect piece. We all live with our own strengths and weaknesses. What we do with these, describe our destiny.

It is imperative to know both your strengths and weakness. Knowing your strengths and using it as tool helps you to carve your path to success. However, it is equally imperative to know your weaknesses; then you can shrug it off. But, that's just not enough. Awareness is the first step and not the only step. There is a proper and scientific approach in working to overcome weaknesses.

Identify your weaknesses—List down all your weaknesses, you think you engross. It may not be one time exercise; you may take few hours to several days to list it down. Be fair to yourselves. You may like to take help of your friends, relatives, parents or even teachers. The list may vary from few to a real exhaustive one. Don't worry about it, just keep adding whatever comes in your view on fair ground and importantly, **don't be panic.**

Accept your weaknesses rather than getting panic or worried about it. We all know that nothing is ideal and perfect in the globe. Overcoming the weaknesses is feasible. How? By observing it and working on it ONE by ONE; not all at once.

You have few in your list; order it down on priority ground, as what is the very first thing you would like to overcome then next and so on. Now pick one or maximum couple of those based on your preferences, frame the corrective action against it and start working on it. I would like to share an example here from my own life. I use to take the extra doses of sleep every day; 9 hrs a day. I realized it as an under utilization of the time and wanted to restrict it to 7hrs. First, I conditioned my mind to achieve my desired goal for few days by repeating my goal every now and then. That way, my mind was in synchronization with what I wanted to achieve. Then I booked one page in my diary to track the number of hours I slept. I had 2 columns on the page; left side column was utilized to mention the date and the corresponding right side column to mention the number of hours I slept for that particular day. I tracked this for more than a month.

Tracking figures displayed initially with the same 9 hours a day. Eventually, it started moving towards the goal for which my mind was conditioned; that is maximum 7 hours of sleep in a day. To achieve this, it took more than a month. What happens is, when you practice certain things, consciously and generously, for quite a long time (Minimum 21days), it then gets inculcated in your blood. You are done! You do not have to look back again.

> On the way to overcoming your weaknesses, you will feel the flow of positive energy within and rise in the confidence.

This way, pick the elements (one by one not all at once), you want to overcome; be it an ill habits like procrastination, laziness, criticizing habit etc or unconscious attitude like ego, jealous, aggressiveness etc., then lay down the corrective action plan and finally, start working on it; if possible track your progress, this will maintain your momentum and keep you motivated on your way to overcome your own weaknesses.

On the way to overcoming your weaknesses, you will feel the flow of positive energy within and rise in the confidence.

Farming Success

L ife is not an instant coffee; you press the button on a machine and your cup is ready with your drink in few seconds. Life is like farming;

> You have to keep patience while you doing the right things.

you need to have patience to wait for crop to pop up and must have wisdom to incorporate appropriate processes and ingredients like seeds, fertilizers, water etc. You also do need the right tools and implements to farm the crop; like tractor, harrow, cultivator, harvester etc.

We all know the basic requirements for farming are—

1. You need to have a fertile land
2. You should have a desired seed
3. You have to cultivate the land before you sow the seed

4. Then sow the seed
5. Apply necessary fertilizers, water, pesticides etc. in between
6. Keep repeating step no 5 at regular interval of time
7. Once the crop is ready, it is now time to harvest it

The crucial point here is charging the patience between cultivating and harvesting. You have to keep patience while you keep doing the right things. Imagine, if farmer gets frustrated in between the process; will he be ever in a position to farm and reap the crops from the seeds he sowed?

Now, let's look the above in the holistic perspective of our life.

1. What is that fertile land—it is the belief system we carry. What we believe makes our mind either fertile or barren.
2. Desired Seed—What you want to become?
3. Cultivate the land—Why you want that and how are you going to achieve it?
4. Sowing the seed—When you are convinced on what, why and how; then it is time to act.
5. Application of fertilizer, water, pesticide etc—On the course of journey, you will have to keep yourself protected from negative influences so you have to keep feeding your mind with

positive energy, which works as pesticide, to create a barrier for negative thoughts. Visualize your dream; imagine yourself doing what you dream of doing. This will work as fertilizer, meaning, it will help you grow by providing the inner motivation.

6. Keep watering yourself with positive thoughts so that your motivation and inspiration keep growing.

7. Once you achieve your dream, cheer yourself up; celebrate it, feel it, enjoy it. Do not postpone your celebration for another achievement and that's what most of the time we do; we keep the celebration for the next achievement.

8. Farmer after celebrating crop harvesting (Lodhi—A harvesting festival in India), get sets for another season. The same way you should also pen down another goal.

The key tools which you require to farm success are vision and determination.

Start with Enthusiasm, Finish with patience.

*T*his is a Story of a 30 yrs old hardworking and a dedicated carpenter. There was a carpenter working with one of the house building company in

> If you are committed to end any project of your life with the same energy, you started with; you are bound to produce the finest output of your life.

a small town. Whatever work he used to pick on his way, his approach was to give 100% to it; as a result he could deliver the finest piece of product. The wooden houses which he built were clearly outstanding in the town. Because of his finest output, word of mouth got spread to adjacent towns and his company started getting contracts from other towns as well. Because of his sincerity and loyalty, he became the asset for his organization. His colleagues and master used to respect him for his dedication. The company's business grew multifolds in few years. As a result, he even bagged good bonuses every year and of course, he was also enjoying an *equally lucrative salary. The chain of his dedication, sincerity and loyalty towards his work and the company continued for 20 years. In his tenure of service, he built numerous houses and furniture, and no one could match his workmanship and finishing.*

Finally, a day came when he decided to retire and spend time with his family. He had enough saving to spend the rest of his retired life in peace. He declared his intention to his master. His master was upset hearing the news of his retirement. He tried to convince him to work with him for another couple of years but in vain. He then made a final request to the carpenter to build one last house with furniture for him in the very same town. Carpenter agreed to his final request and as per the instruction, he started working on it the very next day.

Since, this was his last project; he did not put the complete heart and soul into the project. He was working half heartedly. The materials which he used were not of the top quality. His focus was only to finish the work as soon as possible so that he can have the leisure time of retirement soon after the final project. Even while working on it, most of the time, he was thinking of the post retirement activities. As a result, the finishing of the house and the furniture was not even 50% of what he used to build. But he was now not bothered of it anymore, as it was his last project.

The day came, when the project was ready. He happily went to his master and handed over the keys of the house. The master than smiled at him and handed over the keys back to him as a token of appreciation from him. The

71

carpenter was shocked. He built hundreds of those in his career with utmost finishing and of highest quality. But the one which he built for himself was of inferior quality and ill finished. He was now regretting for not giving the same input in his last project, which he was known for.

This is what mostly happens with most of us. We start with full enthusiasm, do well at the onset; but when it comes to touch the finishing line, we get complacent. This is the phase when we compromise with our ethics and discipline. The moment we put them aside, our output gets affected, no matter whether we are doing it for the first or the last time. You study hard throughout the year but the moment you compromise with the discipline or the ethics just before or during the exams, you may lose the race. You did very well in the first couple of appraisals in your company; then you started relaxing, thinking that you already have marked the impression and set a good track record. This past good record will now guide rest of your journey. And there you bound to decline.

If you are committed to start any project of your life with the full enthusiasm and end it with patience; you are bound to produce the finest output of your life.

ACE NO. 2

ATTITUDE

Talent Vs Attitude

Talent and Attitude when go hand in hand; success can't go far away.

> To grow, we certainly need talent; but to sustain there, we need the right attitude.

In most of the instances, where there is a talent, there arises an attitude. Talent after covering certain distance in a path of success; ceases to derive an excelling. There comes a role of an Attitude.

Talent opens a gate of success for you but an attitude keeps you there.

There was a wood cutter, called Ram; he used to cut trees for one of the company in his town. His job was to cut trees and then split it into pieces of required sizes. He was known for his efficiency and highest productivity. Therefore, he was the highest paid employee, fetching rupees 2000 a month. The company was growing and needed more wood cutters to be employed. The company then hired another wood cutter, named Shyam, at a salary of rupees 1500 a month. The star wood cutter, Ram used to cut 4 trees a day, which was the highest ever number any wood cutter achieved so far. Shyam started cutting 3 trees a day; then a week later; he started cutting 4 trees a day. A month passed by and Shyam was consistent in cutting 4 trees a day. Looking at his productivity, owner decided to pay him same salary as of Ram's, that was rupees 2000 a month. On the other hand, Ram was still at his very stagnant output, 4 trees a day. Since company was growing and wanted more productivity from its employees, an incentive was declared that any one, who cuts 5 trees a day, he will get an incentive of rupees 500 a month. The announcement created a buzz within the employees; but no one had any clue on how to do that. Ram commented that after giving the best, he could only cut 4 trees a day. In case, if 5 trees needed to be cut, then they have to work overtime; this may not be feasible round the month. Shyam was too excited with the announcement. He planned and soon he became the one, who was easily withdrawing an incentive on top of his salary. His boss asked him a favour of training other people as well, which he agreed. Under his guidance, efficiency of others also got bounced up. They were cutting only 3 trees a day and now reached to 4 trees a day. Ram, being senior, refused to take his help and his ego did not allow him to get trained from his junior. Instead, he decided to work harder by giving an extra time, cutting off from the break and lunch time, to cut extra trees. This gave him a boost to cut 5 trees a day but could not sustain it for long and couple of months later; he slipped back to his original performance.

Time passed in a flash and there went 6 months. Now, most of the wood cutters reached to a level where they were able to cut 5 trees a day. They were also very happy to work with Shyam; he was a great team player. He not only helped others to make more money but also continuously improved his own performance. Due to team cohesiveness and satisfaction, the productivity of the company and so as the profits started shooting the top row of the graph. The owner awarded Shyam with an increment of another rupees 500 a month. This made Ram furious than ever. He even claimed salary hike from his boss, which was refused. But by then, he was fair enough to relieve his egoistic approach and accepted Shyam as a better worker than him. He sadly & hesitantly approached Shyam; he confessed that in competition & jealousy, he did not accept his guidance. He also told Shyam that he worked very hard to improve his performance but could not sustain it; then how come he managed to continuously improve his performance along with training others. Shyam was kind enough to share his best practice and secret with him. He said that every time he cut a tree, he spend few minutes in sharpening his axe. This reduces the time and effort to cut the next tree and thereby increases the efficiency. That's what he trained his peers; 'how to sharp axe rather than how to cut trees'. And then few minutes he used to spend in sharing the lighter moments with them, like cracking jokes so that they feel energetic. Ram was amazed to learn these simple tricks.

Ram had talent but Shyam was a master of both talent and the right attitude. That gave him an edge over others and appeared as a splendid leader. To grow, we certainly need talent; but to sustain there, we need the right attitude as well. Ram could reach to his peak but could not sustain himself there; because he did not have the right attitude of learning; rather he was overwhelmed by his own talent. As a result, ego took over the charge. When ego controls us, we miss to value the resources and we focus only on sources. Ram missed to value the learning (resource) from Shyam and his focus was to consider him (source) as his junior, and there his ego did not allow to learn from him.

A Study Attributed to Harvard University found that a person gets success, 85% of the time because of his Attitude and only 15% of the time because of his skills, qualifications or knowledge of some facts and figures. Surprisingly, yet 100% of the education dollars goes into the teaching of facts and figures, which accounts for only 15% of success in life!

Focused and Smart approach will act as catalyst; while, Talent and Attitude as ingredients to Success.

Law of Peace

Nature has its own laws and one of the laws suggests that what you give will come back to you in manifold. You sow a seed and

> One of the core reasons why people get jealous of each other or hate each other is because they feel they are in a competition with each other

you will not get just one flower or a fruit; you will get many. If you spread love in the air, it will come back to you densely. The same applies to detestation. The kind of energy you reflect, it will come back to you multiple times. You hate someone and at the same time, you can't feel happy and relaxed. You criticize others and still can't emit positive energy. If you are not emitting happiness or positivity, your soul will never be in peace.

By appropriately and wisely making your choices, you can either rest your soul in peace or keep on dealing with restlessness, which finally cooks the frustration within you. If you follow the law of giving and receiving, you will explore another law linked with it, The Law of Peace, which says—

1. Don't radiate negative energy in any form. Love people, look at them as if they are your well wishers; love the situations you come across, look at it as if it has some great message for you. Be happy with other's successes; do not get jealous of it. Success will not come to you if you radiate negative energy for success, doesn't matter, even if it is for others' success. So don't get jealous with others success, cheer it. Cheer today in others' success, be a part of their happiness, you may also need someone to cheer for you in your success. Life works in a circular form, not in a straight line. You will come across the same point after every rotation. If you paint every exiting point with peace and happiness, you will enjoy the very same flavor, when you cross that point in your next turn. On the other hand if you fill it with jealousy or hatred, you will be propounded with jealousy/ hatred that you left in your previous rotation and that too in multifold, as stated earlier.

2. One of the core reasons why people get jealous of each other or hate each other is because they feel they are in a competition with each other. They feel that life is a race and they have to win it. If they have to win, they have to leave their competitors behind. Life is not like a race, where only one wins. Life is

like a team of football or hockey or cricket, where the entire team wins. Take it this way that the entire world is part of your team and you are competing with the team of adversity. What do you do? You cooperate with your team players, work in synchronization and beat the other team. That's what we have to do here. We have to cooperate with each human being, be it your family members, colleagues, neighbors or any stranger and we should help each other to beat the adversity. Today, you co-operate and help someone to beat the adversity he faces; tomorrow someone will help you to defeat the adversity you face. In summary, transform competition into cooperation. This transformation will dwell peace within.

3. I got to understand the connection of peace and sharing quite a long ago. I was working part time on a commission basis to support my livelihood; while pursuing higher studies, so that my expenses should not be a burden for my parents. Anyways, every time I used to get commission on my work, I used to share some part of it with the needy; albeit, the pay checks of the commission were not even sufficient to fulfill my own needs. Even though, I didn't know why I use to do that; but one thing was for sure; I used to have a feeling of immense satisfaction. Sharing is not a new concept; however this is a widely ignorant concept. By

> Sharing is not a new concept; however this is a widely ignorant concept.

this article, I would like to emphasize that sharing is as crucial as receiving.

Share whatever you can; be it—

A. Happiness—bring a smile on others face by cracking a joke, helping them to forget their sorrows and get energized for next challenge.

B. Inspiration—motivate and inspire others. Share successful examples with them to give directions to their lives.

C. Money—There are so many students who are not able to pursue higher studies, poor who can't feed their children, homeless people—who are bound to spend nights on the pavement of the street because they do not have sufficient money for it; charity them.

D. Time—Share time with your kids and elderly people at home, they need your attention. Spare some time to help others, devote some time for religious causes. Spare some time in contributing towards the development of society, etc.

Sharing is all about gaining, not loosing; gaining peace and satisfaction.

To summarize, The Law of Peace works on 3 key principles—

1. Radiation—Radiate positive energy
2. Transformation—Transform competition to cooperation
3. Sharing—Happiness, Inspiration, Money and Time; Share to Receive.

Inner voice

The whole day, your inner voice whispers to you. You listen to it or not, but it keep sharing something with you. You may like it or you

The whole day, your inner voice whispers to you. You listen to it or not, but it keep sharing something with you.

may refuse to accept it; but it keeps buzzing within. No matter how loud is the external world, your inner voice will still be whispering gently. It never forces you to listen to it but the choice is left to you. The doors are always open from that side; you can head back anytime. The inner peace will always have arms open for you. When you do not find something, which you are badly gunning at; you can return back to inner peace and your inner voice will guide you the right path. That's something proven and widely accepted. But then why one fail to listen to it?

In this chaotic lifestyle, we often forget to record our inner voice and are more likely to be driven by the opinion of others. The religious gurus, boss, colleagues, friends, unknown starring eyes; these all start influencing you when you are not connected with your own soul and the spiritual cable that connects us with our soul is none other than 'Inner Voice'. The internal dialogue is very crucial, that comes out of the selfless resources. The objective of this resource is to tell you a truth, merely truth. Listening to inner voice will blunt the attack of external negative influences.

It is a good idea to record your inner voice. You may like to pen down what is floating in your inner side or may even make the best use of technology, record it in your smart phone or any other recording devices. Whenever a thought spark in my mind or inner dialogue begins, I record it in my voice in my cell phone. Later, I review it. Do not worry; just keep recording, what comes out from your deep inside. You may also pen it down in your diary or journal. Believe me, when you start reviewing your inner voice, you will be surprised with the output in the form of ideas, solutions to your worries, attitude development conversations. Believe me, it has solutions and answers to all worries and circumstances. No teacher or priest can teach you, what your inner conscience can do. It provides you the sense of proportion.

I started recording my inner dialogue in my journal when I was in 1st year of my engineering in 1997. I started writing my daily briefings on what happened that day, the kind of emotions I passed through, my achievements for the day etc. Then, over the period of time, surprisingly, the daily buzzing words started taking shape of the words of wisdom flowing from the deep inside. In the very next step, I found myself recording the broader inner dialogues encompassing the circumstances or scenarios faced with the suggested actions, dealing with emotions that helped developing my emotional intelligence (EQ). The sense of proportion was quiet evident and I could clearly glimpse between the tough time slots, I faced during my teenage due to ill financial and emotional backup. This ability to develop the wisdom would have been possible, as I was in complete discipline in spending more than 30 minutes every day, engaging myself in inner dialogues. Even today, when I look back at those thoughts and inner dialogues, it boosts my emotions positively.

> Believe me, things will start changing on your side, when you deal with the thoughts you hold inside.

Inner voice is the powerful piece of tool available with all humans since birth and yet not explored well. Listen to it; play a game with it and the rules of the game are—

1. Time—Minimum 15 minutes game everyday till rest of your life.
2. Number of Players—Only one player required and allowed; and that is you.

3. Ground / Pitch—Of your choice; be it circumstances, emotions, worries, goals, self commitment etc

4. Winner—The match is fixed; you will be the winner always.

Believe me, things will start changing on your side, when you deal with the thoughts you hold inside. Do not suppress it with ego, self esteem, greed, others' opinion, etc. Listen to your inner voice as pure soul.

Every human being is sent in this world by that supreme power with a gift (Inner Voice). Whenever you expect a gift from God in any given circumstances, open this gift box and you will be surprised to receive what you wanted.

I choose to listen to my inner voice and not just the opinion of others.

What are you going to listen today?

Testing inner strength

Facing and handling difficult time is a part of the game for all lives; be it a mankind or an animal.

> How we react in an unfavourable condition; reveals our thought process ideology and inner strength.

In fact, animals are found to be more positive reactor than humans under unfavourable circumstances. When animals, birds or any species run through some crises for food, water or shelter, they move off in search of another location, where they can fulfil their needs. Whereas, in case of any mental, physical or economical crises; the basic tendency of human mind is to sit and creep. Rarely, people have an ideology to shift their attention immediately for the solutions. Unfortunately, most of us get fatigue focusing on problems and failures. They forget the saying, which we might have heard numerous times in our life, which tell us that the test of courage is to bear the defeat without losing our heart.

How we react in an unfavourable condition; reveals our thought process, ideology and inner strength. This is when we can judge our bar of internal strength / personality. Once we know where we stand on the graph, we can plan the required actions to ensure the peak point representation of our personality.

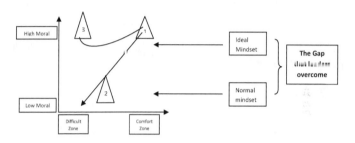

The above graph suggests that when we are at a comfort zone, our moral is high, which is quiet apparent. Contrary, as and when the situation gets difficult, our motivation starts sliding down. As a part

of normal human tendency, the bar will go down, but the one whose bar bounced back to attain the high moral, even during the tough time, surely emerges as a leader.

Now, the point is how? The magic is "positive thinking".

Staying with a positive mindset all throughout; calls for potentially huge energy level for the brain. Research shows that when we are surrounded by negative thoughts, it takes down our energy and power of the brain to stay positive; but when the brain is fed with tons of positive thoughts, energy bar starts

shooting again back to attain the peak. $\triangle$ 3

A physician suggests supplements or lots of fruits, juices, vegetables etc. when a patient is suffering from lack of iron, calcium or vitamins in his body to get back the lost rhythm of the body. Similarly, to get back the rhythm of the mind, the supplements are only positive thoughts.

Once the positive thoughts are blended with positive actions, the outcome would not just be the success; but it could be miracle as well.

You go and check out anyone, who has done great things in their lives has made it feasible by blending positive thoughts with the positive actions; be he a great Mahatma Gandhi, Bollywood Star Shahrukh Khan, Boxer—Mohammad Ali, Cricketer—Sachin Tendulkar or Leader—Barack Obama.

Peer Pressure

This article is about the peer pressure which we all sail through; however teenagers are more prone to get attacked and affected by it.

> Teen years are base of your life. What you develop here will have a lifelong impact. Your choice defines your destiny.

What is Peer Pressure? To understand it, let us break this and define these two words separately— Peer and Pressure.

Peer is your friend, a person of your age group in your school, college, sports club, community etc.

Pressure is the force you develop within, to imitate the actions and decisions of your peers, especially the ones who are close to you.

When you were a kid, your parents used to choose friends and play group for you. You would be allowed to play with only those kids, whom they deemed fit for you. As you grew, you started choosing your own group, depending on the common interests and attitude. On daily basis, we all take certain decisions, based on the influences from each other. For example, one of your friend bought a new sporty look bike or trendy jeans, which you find attractive; you might too like to own one. Another common example which I observed during my teenage was, choosing the degree level course or college, post the basic schooling, based on what peer choose. I heard people mentioning that I want to pursue Engineering, as most of my batch mates are gunning for it. To add further, "my friends are filing a form for admission in Mechanical Engineering, so as I."

As you grow, you happen to spend more time with your peers than with your family members. Unknowingly and unintentionally, you start depending on your peers to take decisions. Here, you get the real introduction of 'Peer Pressure' in your life. Teen Peer Pressure often comes from within. You often generate internal pressure to copy your peers; may be dressing like him or her, securing good marks like him/her etc., so that you are accepted by them. You happen to develop an internal pressure to ensure the approval and acceptance by your peers. This pressure is powerful and at times may have serious consequences too. Person who are low in confidence often tend to follow others, whereas the one with high confidence stand on his own. However, imitating the good things is positive and adhering on one's own stand (resistance to positive change) can be as a result of ego, which is detrimental to own personality.

So, is it good or bad? Positive or Negative?

In this beautiful world, there is nothing with only one specification or character in it. Every matter in the world has both—'pros and cons', 'good and bad', 'advantage and disadvantage'.

Teen years are tough. This is the phase when you start exploring yourself, your dreams, your strengths, your responsibilities, your challenges, your goals and your belief. Exploring these attributes can put you in a ring of wrestling. However, you can make your journey comfortable by facing the challenges with your friends, who are also sailing on the same boat.

A good group is always encouraging, motivational and provides you strength to face the tough challenges. Peers can set a good example for each other. You can share your experiences, feelings, aspirations etc. comfortably with your peers than with your parents. Most of the time, they act as stress buster and then re-energize you with the fresh energy. Teenagers are easily open to receive the advices from peers. You need to be very careful on the advices you get from your peers and vice versa. Following a good advice can make you and on contrary, getting influenced by ill advice can break you for your lifetime. Positive recommendations or criticism from your peers helps you to develop skills and attitude. They encourage you from time to time, develop social skills and inculcate positive thought process in you.

On the other side, association of pernicious (harmful) group can altogether have adverse effects in your life. You need to be extra vigilant in choosing your peers and groups. Teens' decisions are highly influenced by peers group and are more likely to copy each other; intentionally or unintentionally. A study by researchers at Columbia University shows that kids are six times more likely to drink alcohol if their friends do the same.

I would suggest a very important and at the same time, most ignorant aspect. Teenagers mostly do not share their peer activities with parents. As a result, parents do not have clear perspective on the direction you are heading with your group. It is advisable that you should share at least 3 things of your peers with your parents fairly—

1) What you like about your friends,
2) What you don't like about them, and
3) What can you learn from them

I strongly feel, with this, your parents will be able to help you to suggest if you are in right group.

When I was in teen age, I faced an objection from my parents on my association to a group of my peers; they forcefully moved me from the group. That badly hurted me. I literally cursed them for this act. Few years later, when I looked back, I was ashamed of my cursing to my well wishers (parents), as most of the peers from that group headed to a direction, which no society will appreciate.

To summarize, peer pressure in most of the cases, is positive and help us to get energy, positivity and direction. It helps us in developing various skills including social skill. A good group can help each other in setting goals of their lives as well. However, be careful in choosing your peer group; share with your parents fairly about your group and rely on their feedback.

A long lasting structure is the outcome of the strong foundation. Teen years are base of your life. What you develop here will have a lifelong impact. Your choice defines your destiny.

Small achievements, Big success

I am not going to talk big in this article. I will share small and yet very important things. It is imperative to first master small steps before

> Even a biggest success doesn't exist at its own, there are smaller successes which together takes a shape of big success.

you take the leap. We all know that a leopard is the fastest animal on the planet. Have you ever noticed that before he really takes a leap, he starts with small steps, which then he quickly converts it to a big one and then finally takes a giant leap?

It is therefore said that the journey of thousands miles begins with a small step.

A day before yesterday when I reached back home after a chaotic day, I badly wanted few minutes of relaxation. My 8 years old son was eagerly waiting for my arrival and as soon as I entered; he jumped on me. He started sharing about what he got to know about atoms that day. He is a curious boy and loves to explore various subjects of science. I was seriously not in a good tempo to listen but at the same time I did not want to discourage his enthusiasm; so starred at him as if I am listening to him with full attention. He started blasting with his study on atoms with full throttle of enthusiasm. He explained it in a simpler form that triggered me something very interesting. I will like to put his words on how he explained it," Everything in the world is made of lot many atoms. Atoms are small particles. Inside the atoms, there is a bag like thing, called nucleus, which contains protons and neutrons; they are positive (positively charged). Electrons are negative (negatively charged) that is why they do not stay with protons and neutrons and rotates outside nucleus. Then he finally added that nothing in the world exists without having atoms in it, even big mountains are made of very small atoms."

This inspired me a lot. This theory is very relevant in our life; even a biggest success doesn't exist at its own, there are smaller successes which together takes a shape of big success. Wright brothers, when took their first flight on 17th December 1903, it lasted only 12 seconds for a total distance of 120 feet and today only a wing span of a Boeing 747 is 195 feet. This big invention is a result of that small success. Because of that short flight of 12 seconds, now we can enjoy continuous flights of hours in safety and comfort.

Accumulate your every small achievement; cheer it, celebrate it and make it a part of your bigger success. Many of us tend to ignore the small achievements of our lives. We are ignorant of their values and contribution to big success. Achieved a degree or a master degree, bought a new bicycle or a car, spent good weekend with your family, gone for a dinner with your wife on your anniversary, donated a coin for a charity; are all perfectly legitimate forms of success. These small successes will overall take a shape of some big success. You got a master degree, now you can either pursue further higher studies or take a job, which in turn will help you to grow more. Until now you were commuting by local transport and now you bought a bicycle, bike or a car; with this you can cover your distance faster and now can save some time to invest in achieving your goals. Spending good time with your family will give you peace and energize you with happiness, which works as fuel and this energy can then be utilized in achieving your dreams. Every such small achievement is having direct relationships with your bigger picture. So do not underestimate your small successes.

> Every such small achievement is having direct relationships with your bigger picture. So do not underestimate small successes.

Remember, even giant mountains are even made up of smaller particles called atoms.

Fail to Succeed

Failure OR Success is finding out what does or doesn't work. The choice is yours, how you look at it.

> Formula is a logical form not an emotional form. The results will always be the same, if the conditions are same.

Thousands times, it has been heard that failures are key to success. You go and check out anybody, who has done anything in life, has marked his success by identifying what doesn't work and exploring the new ways to do it.

Cricketer at times fails to play a ball of particular length in a right way and gets out of the field. A good batsman doesn't give up there, he explores the ways to attack and counteract such kind of deliveries while practicing. Will you tag him as a failure?

When you cook something for the first time, you might either get the food over cooked or under cooked; salt missed to be added as per the taste or cooked it too spicy. You then tag your mistake and discover the correct approach to cook your dish, right?

You might think here that you can't relate the failures in cooking with that in career or something that affects your life drastically. Failure in cooking doesn't kill you but if you fail in your business, studies or relationships, it will have a greater impact on your morale.

If you notice, the formula for "success from failure" is same, irrespective of situations. Formula is a logical form; not an emotional form. The results will always be the same, if the conditions are same. No matter who applies it, men or women, child or adult, worker or manager, etc and where is it applied, in business or relationships. What you do is, you rate the size of the failures from non significant to critical. Failure in cooking is insignificant; while in relationship, it is critical. The moment you rate the size of the failure, you lose trust on the effectiveness of this formula; as a result of which you surrender and certify yourself as victim.

Let's study the formula;

Success (Output)
=Total ingredients (Input)—ingredients of failures

Input is variable, which is, what you did in order to derive the output (success). Post your attempt(s), when the desired results are not arrived, discover the reason(s) for failure and deduct it from your input in next try.

A batsman discovered after he got out on a particular length of ball that he should have played the ball straight rather than tilting the face of the bat to play it in on or off side of the field. After you spoilt the food, you got to learn that it should have been cooked for 15 minutes rather than for 25 minutes. What you did here, you discarded the ingredients leading to failures from your total ingredients of input.

This applies with every situation, be it a business, career or relationships. Just explore the ingredients of failures and remove it from the input and there you are ready with another recipe of success. Be motivated to repeat the same practice, till you derive the desired outcome (success).

Albert Einstein said that it is insanity, if you are doing the same thing over and over again and yet expecting the different results.

Most of you have heard about failures of highly successful personalities like Bill Gates, Wright brothers, Albert Einstein, Thomas Edison and so on. However, I would like to share my failures which helped me to reach where I am today. But before that I will share a background of my life.

I am from a middle class family, had an education in state boards from C class city of India. I wanted to pursue engineering but did not score well in 12th grade; as a result I did not get admission in conventional engineering colleges. Incidentally, I happened to clear the entrance test for Aircraft Maintenance Engineering and proudly pursued it with the help of scholarship and some financial support from local educational bodies. Since my father expired, when I was in 11th grade and being the eldest child, the responsibilities and morale pressure was high on me. Anyways, the journey of my failures and struggle started after I completed Aircraft Maintenance Engineering. I had to get a job so that first I can be financially independent and later I can take the responsibilities of my family, so that I can put full stop on my mother's hard work.

I can proudly say that I came long way to where I am from where I was. But there were numerous failures and abundant struggle encountered in the journey. I have listed below few of them with learning I was propounded.

1. **Didn't get job in Aviation**—I passed engineering with a very good score. I was all set to fly high. But the real shade of life turned out to be darker, which was beyond imagination. Even after scrolling from one airline's office to another; searching for job by turning pages of one news paper to other, for months, I stood with bare hands. My morale started touching the ground. With no financial back up, I had to accept the failure. With heavy heart, I migrated to sales job in order to survive.

After 14 years, when I find that there are now very few airlines in India; and that too in struggling phase; we all know recent scenario of mergers and complete collapse of airlines. When I imagine now; if I would have been absorbed in aviation industry that time, I probably would have been facing slow growth or stuck at one position and could not even shift the industry. I am now a free bird; changed 7 jobs in 14 years. I started my career on commission basis, was earning not even Rs 2000 a month in Delhi then shifted to a job where I was getting salary of Rs 3500 in the year 2000 and today in 13yrs time, I am getting a monthly salary, which is more than 10 times of my annual salary in 2000.

2. *I had to bear the extremes of weather of New Delhi by walking more than 10 kms. one way to office, to save a bus fare of Rs 2—*
   It used to take more than an hour to reach to New Delhi Railway station from Karolbagh. I had to bear extremes of weather but that was very good time to spend with one self. I used to talk within a lot. When you talk positively with yourself, you find solutions to problems. The solution to my struggle was to keep focus on the goal and that self talk helped me to do that. It helped me gain the wisdom by listening to inner voice. If I could manage to write a book, that 10 kms daily walk has a big contribution in this.

3. *Rejected for a position of Sales Executive, in an interview from a local lubricants manufacturer in New Delhi in the year 2000*—
I remember well, before going for an interview, I studied the company and the products a bit and during the interview, they asked me how I can contribute to their company. I gave few fundamentals on the research I did, pointing the issues in sales and visibility of the products in the market, without knowing that the person sitting in front of me was the sales manager for the region. My recommendations slammed his ego and he reacted so badly and thrown a hurting statement on my face. I still remember what he said that you are no one in front of me; YOU ARE ZERO. And, 5 years later I was working with one of the best lubricant company in the world—Castrol. What I learnt there is, encompassing knowledge is good but at the same time, you need to have a wisdom to use your knowledge.

4. *Rejected in an interview with one of the world class call center in New Delhi in the year 2000*—
That was the time when youngsters were getting hired by the top call centers at a lucrative salary and splendid ambience to work. Not just commerce or arts graduates, even engineers were also getting attracted towards the job in call

center as an executive, of course due to salary and working environment, which was not there in most of the hard core engineering jobs those days. I got through with the telephonic interview but got rejected in 3rd round of selection process in group discussion. I got upset and cried a little as I badly wanted that job to excel in life and support myself. Today, we all know that the call center industry is struggling. It was a high rise bubble of just few years and unfortunately, professionals from that industry struggled a lot later. If I would have got selected there, my career would have been something else. Not just that, that failure shook me from bottom to top. I bought a book on group discussion and tried to learn the basics of it so as to add that skill in me. I admit that it helped me beyond my expectations. I just bought the book to get ready for another interview for call center. But behaving and reacting in group is something very crucial in your career and it is even helping me now.

5. **Rejected in another interview in 2nd round of selection process with one of the reputed Indian player of automotive components in the year 2001 in Mumbai—**

I cleared the first round of interview in Delhi for the position of sales engineer; then I was called to Mumbai for the final selection process. I was asked to meet to a Regional Sales Manager. After general interaction, he asked me to sell him a pen from his desk. While trying to do that he came with lots of objections in buying the pen. I tried to come with the different propositions to mark a sale, but I could not sell it to him virtually. And while trying to sell that pen, I handled the objections in such a silly way that today I laugh at it. I was then out of the race. I was very upset and went to a church in Bandra that night and then to Bandstand (a place in Mumbai). I sat near a sea shore right opposite Shahrukh Khan's (Bollywood superstar) bungalow (as I stayed in Bandra with my cousin). I spent couple of hours alone. The self conversation started with depression and frustration. With empty eyes, I looked back and starred at Saharukh's bungalow that boosted me with calories of energy; may be because he is one of them who attained the fame not as a gift from family but earned hard way. Thoughts then started excelling to constructive direction. Rather than creeping, I decided to understand the reasons for failure (ingredients of failure). I started working on selling skills; read theories, discussed with the professionals in field, watched documentaries around it and did whatever I could to understand the basics of selling. Wherever I worked, I implemented the theories on selling skills I learnt and kept exploring it further along, by developing new ones. In my career so far, out of 14 years; I am in sales for the last 10 years. And in last 10 years, I have bagged 8 times best performance awards in sales. Not just that, I have even won various high level sales incentives and competitions.

6. *Left Job in an anxious way without having backup source of income-*

I worked while studying, with one of the property developers in Delhi, where I used to work 10 hrs a day (10-8 pm) and 7 days a week. Even for working so hard, I was just getting Rs 3500 a month. I limited my expenses to Rs 3000 only and out of it, I used to put Rs 500 in saving. Due to high dissatisfactory conditions, I left the company without thinking much; however by taking a calculated risk. By that time, I had a saving of Rs 9,000 and my monthly expenses were within Rs 3000; so I could then survive for 3 months without job. I took risk as I completed my AMIAE and started looking for job in the industry badly and madly. I appeared in walk in interviews, posted CVs, did cold callings; I did whatever I could. In few weeks, I got an interview call letter from Ceat Tyres for the position of Territory Manager. I got shocked as I was gunning only for sales executive/ sales engineer position, as I did not have enough experience for managerial position.

I was out of confidence for that position and I didn't turn up. Knowing this, my mother was upset so as my girl friend (now my wife). But both of them boosted me. Anyways, a month later, I got a call one morning at my landlord's number. This call was from an HR department of Ceat. Asking if I can make for the interview now? I grabbed this opportunity without being foolish this time and headed for an interview, as per the agreed schedule. Out of 12-15 candidates, I got selected and that was the turning point of my career and struggle. After that break, I did not have to look back.

If I would not have taken that calculated risk and left that company, which was not in my career track, I would have been in other circumstances this time. You have to take a risk in your life and that has to be calculated.

7. **Debt of 4.75 lacs—pushed me to take a job in UAE, by compromising a bit in profile—**

Everything was going good. I jumped from an organization to another; the market was booming so as the salary packages were. But because of some ill finance planning and monitoring, my debt bar was raising. And by 2008, I was already in a debt of Rs 4.75 lacs. This would have taken years for me to just bring it to the zero level; forget about saving for future. I then got a call from one of the leading MNC in Lubricants for the job in UAE. I had to compromise at my profile for a package with reasonably good saving potential. In first 6 months I cleared my debt and came to zero position—no saving and no debt. Then from there, steadily and slowly my bank balance started shooting up. It was more than 3 years with that organization and I was then financially comfortable. Now again it was time to take a calculated risk and get the profile back, which I compromised to attain the financial objectives. So I started looking for a desired job profile. After struggling a bit, I got a regional profile and now I am handling business in 6 countries of Middle East. I failed in attaining my financial objectives, even though I could. And in order to get a life back on track, I had to trade my profile and compromise on my career move. This failure, albeit turned out to be blessings in disguise but taught me a great lesson of financial freedom. I am today cautious about my financial planning and by the grace of God; I am now well placed because of it.

Failures are upsetting; I do agree. But the lessons slouches there are 'Up Setting'. It is meant to raise your bar, it is meant to set you up, it is meant to fly you high.

Failures are actually the Path of Success. It's okay to fail, in order to succeed.

ACE NO. 3

ATTRIBUTES

Praise to Raise

Praising is a need, more than an art.

I always suffered in relationships during my school and college days. I could not gel with every one; as a result I had few friends. More or less, the situation was same even when I was in my professional path. I thought, it might be because of my reserved nature. It took ages for me to understand one missing dot here, due to which the whole picture was not been plotted.

The missing dot was about creating an influential surrounding around self. Knowingly or unknowingly, people love to be in association with someone who influences them. Influencing is basically raising someone's aspiration and making them feel worth. There are 3 sets of people; one who love criticizing; second, who believe in praising & appreciating; and third, who refrain themselves from passing any comments, be it praising or criticizing.

Needless to say that people from category one are the destroyers, category two are creators and third category are spectators. Criticizing destroys, praising influences positively and being just spectating is of mere help to anyone. I was in third category. Since, I was exhibiting no or little values to others, I had few followers; very obvious!

It took ages for me to understand this simple equation of creating followers and having healthier relationships. Appreciating and praising is not a new concept; however it is one of the most ignorant concepts. Not just that, it even help us to contribute to the community indirectly.

When we praise someone, we make them feel worth. Appreciate your child for something, appreciate your wife or mother for the efforts they put in to maintain the house, appreciate your father for his hard efforts in supporting needs of the members, appreciate your friends for helping someone, appreciate your teachers for their guidance, even appreciate your servants for their services etc. Every time you praise someone, you raise them; you raise their motivation, you raise their capability, you raise their belief and you in turn raise their productivity.

When we raise an individual, we raise a family; when families are raised, a society is raised; when societies are raised, city is raised; and this can be extrapolated to the country level. This way by raising individuals, we can make the world a better place to live.

There are few principles of praising. These are—

1. Legitimate—Be sure that your praises are in legitimate form; it should not be with an intention to achieve in return.
2. Specific—Don't be generic like "Good work", "Excellent speech", "Nice Car". Let the person know the specific thing or action you like; what you like about his work, what were the strong components of her speech, what were the features of the car you got attracted with.
3. Reason—It is good to provide the reason why you like the specific action, behavior or thing and the impact it may have.
4. Comparison—Do not compare with others when you praise. People have tendency to raise someone by putting others down. That's not a fair practice. By actually doing this, you will be diluting the purpose of praising.

Benefits of Praising—

When you praise, it's not just the other person receive something; you too are at recipient end.

To Self—

1. You radiate positive energy; and this creates an energetic and influential energy around you.
2. People will love to be in association with you.

3. You will be respected; remember that gaining respect is more difficult than earning money.
4. Your self confidence will be increased.
5. You too learn a lot on the course of praising and giving positive feedback

To others—

1. Their moral will be high.
2. Self confidence will be boosted.
3. They will be aware of their strengths.
4. They will be aware of the impact of their actions.
5. They can be more responsible towards self and society.
6. They even can be comfortable in appreciating others; thereby the chain of praising can be continued to benefit the mass.

When praising becomes dogma; it transforms lives. Praising not just raises others, but also the one who praises. It is a win-win equation.

So seal the deal and praise to raise.

Break the Rules

We are not born with the beliefs, we grow with them. We follow those pre-defined beliefs like a flock of sheep. By following other's

> We are not born with beliefs; we grow with them.

beliefs, you put your efforts on the wrong horse. You need to observe the cause and effect with the transparent lens, not with the perceived lens.

Let's study the evolution pattern of certain belief. The simple formula for deriving output is input (x) times function (f), which is f(x). This means output of anything depends on the input and the function. This formula is not just useful in deriving mechanical outputs but is equally applicable in human mechanism.

We are not casted in the same mold and have the varied capacity, interests, skills, knowledge, preferences and potential (inputs) and therefore every human being is not same; similarly the degrees, at which we utilize these skills and capabilities are way different; it's a David and Goliath situation. When both of these parameters (input and function) are not same all the time, how can the output be the same? We fail to understand this simple logic in our life and starts swallowing our own beliefs. Gradually we keep believing on the output derived by someone, sometime on something and incorporate it in our belief system as another rule of the game.

One day, on my vacation to India, I was having a cup of tea with one of my old school mates in his office. He did his engineering from IIT and after serving few years in leading corporate; he is now running his coaching institute. He is coaching young aspirators to crack IIT and other competitive entrance tests for engineering and management. While we were recollecting some old memories, parents came to my friend's office with his 16 years old son and shown interest in enrolling him to his institute for IIT crack course. My friend asked the boy, "Why you want to go for IIT?" He replied in dull voice," Because my parents want me to do." My friend again asked him," So what you want to do?" The boy looked at his parents and kept silent. His father suddenly jumped between the conversation and said," Actually, my cousin's son is an IIT engineer; he is now abroad and is withdrawing handsome salary; so as a parent, I even want my child to be successful like him. In order to do so, I am ready to pay even hefty fee by borrowing loan." I and my friend looked at each other as if he hit the panic button. My friend signaled me to take a lead in discussion. I engaged boy gently in the conversation," We will help you get prepared for IIT entrance test so don't worry on that front; will that make you very happy, once you get an admission in such a reputed engineering college?" The boy again remained silent for few seconds, while he was looking down with poker face; then he showed a little bit of courage to speak in front of his parents and accepted that he will not be very happy even if he gets an admission in IIT. I slowly dug his interest and asked with a smile on my face," Which career will make you feel happy?" This time, he replied without any hesitation," Singing." Again his father jumped into the conversation and floated his own belief that singing is good for nothing; one can't make career out of it. This industry is limited only to few; not even 1% of strugglers get chance to give a voice in bollywood movies. After silence for few seconds, I gently pulled the thoughts from boy's mind," What will you do, once you become an engineer from IIT?" The boy then said," I will work for few years and then I will open my own recording studio from my savings. I will launch my band and album. I will also open a marketing firm, where I will hire people; their responsibilities will be to bring the aspirated new singers to use my studio facilities to record their own albums. My marketing firm will charge them for using the facility and marketing their albums. I may even hire good singers on contract and together we can organize some events and shows. With this, I can fulfill my own dreams and of other's similar aspirated singers too, who do not have approach to bigger platforms." We all, including his parents, were stunned to listen to a detailed plan from 16 years old boy. While he was describing his plan, his facial expression and body gesture completely shifted from dull to energetic. His parents got the message; his father immediately jumped to him, hugged him and cried. He thanked me that this 10 minutes of discussion saved a life of his son. He was ashamed that due to his own wishes, his son would have to suffer for few years to start his dream project. No parents want their child to suffer in any way because of them. They withdrew their force and allowed his child to break all the rules and to live his life based on his own beliefs.

Sadly, that is the story of almost every second youngster of today. Either they are not cleared what to be done; or if they are then their will is imposed with someone's desires. It is not true that if I am successful as a Sales person then whoever wants to be successful will have to be in sales. Everyone in the world has some unique strength. Then why to speak one's mind?

Some of the common beliefs are—

1. You have to work very hard in order to become successful.
2. If you are born rich, you are powerful and other way round.
3. Sound financial back up means more risk taking capacity.
4. More educational degrees means more knowledge.

Only people who challenged the external belief system could excel in their lives. External belief system is like an invisible boundary created around us; that will not allow us to look beyond that. This boundary is built by our own family members, friends, relatives, society, teachers etc. It is not their fault as well; because they even have brought up with some invisible boundary wall around them since their childhood. So that is the heritage ritual. You can look around for successful people and you will find that they managed to look beyond that invisible boundary or never noticed it.

We heard numerous times that in order to stand out from the crowd, think out of the box; and this box is nothing else but the belief system we follow.

Connecting the Dots

In our childhood, we all indulged into an activity wherein a picture is formed by connecting the dots in sequence. This game is still on even when we are grown up. We, knowingly or unknowingly, are still into the same activity in day to day routine; we connect the dots in sequence. But the game has become bit challenging. The dots are now hidden and you need to identify the dots and sequence in order to connect it to form a picture of success. One, who managed to connect those dots, has become successful in his life.

> Remember, every thought we think is creating our future!

Let's see, what these dots are? And what is the sequence of connecting these dots?

These are Thoughts, Action, Attitude, Habits and Destiny. It is well known fact that thoughts inspire you to act in a certain way; your actions then develops attitude, which in turn gets molded as your habit. And finally, your habit of doing certain thing in a certain way or not doing certain thing at all, sets your destiny.

How thoughts are generated? What is the operating platform that generates thoughts? Is there any way, one can control his/her thoughts? Our thoughts are based on what we believe. Our opinion and reaction depends on the belief system we are grown with. Please note, we are not born with any belief; we grow with them. Religion we follow, society we live in, family we are born in, kind and level of education we have, values we bear; etc. are all the factors responsible for carving our beliefs. And thoughts are the byproducts of those beliefs. We can't change our thoughts without changing the beliefs. It is like, if we have to go to school, we have to step out of our home. The same way, if we want to learn something unconventional; we need to step out of our conventional belief systems.

In a research, a group of people were asked, what success means to them? The responses varied; for some it was acquiring power and money, for others it was happiness, for few it was family & friends and for rest it was spiritual attainment. Why there were different thoughts and opinions to same question? Because the belief systems which they followed were not same!

Now, do you think that everyone in that group will follow the same course of action in order to attain success? Certainly not! People who believed that owning abundance of power and money is success, will act towards achieving it, while on other hand, few who believed that attaining spirituality is the greatest achievement in life, will act to gather spiritual knowledge and follow the spiritual path.

So, the control of our thoughts and actions are in hand of the belief system we follow. And the interesting thing is that this belief system is not formed by our own beliefs; it is designed by someone in the world and we just follow it. It is an external wish and not an internal gift. The questions of an hour here are—Does these belief systems work for us or act against us? Is it feasible to come out of it in case if it doesn't help us? Belief system, itself, is not right or wrong; it differs from one person to another. What worked for me, not necessarily will work for all and vice-versa. We are responsible to control our thoughts and keep check of it. We need to ascertain that whatever thoughts we are playing with are the ones which will help us achieving our very own goal, not the wish of others. We need to incorporate a periodical check system within to identify what we are thinking. Are these thoughts relevant to what I want to achieve? Are these thoughts in line with what is required to be believed in order to bag success? If not then make corrections and bring changes. Repeat the exercise and practice the affirmation consciously. You will be surprised to notice that slowly you started mastering your thoughts unconsciously. Once thoughts are in absolute control of self, one can easily command the actions required to frame the right attitude. These three dots are then well connected.

Let's look at another dot in the sequence; which is Habit. How habits are formed? Of course, it is derived from the actions we perform. Habit is nothing else but the pattern of actions we follow under the same set of circumstances. For instance, I became habitual of listening to music while I sleep; because every night when I go to bed, I first put my music system on with my favorite music tuned in it and then only I can concentrate to sleep. I have conditioned my mind this way by performing a specific task under a specific circumstance. My mind will therefore respond that way effectively. Developing habit is nothing else but the conditioning of your mind.

The bigger question is, can this set pattern of action or conditioning of mind be altered? The answer is YES! You need 'Will and Skill' to change the deep rooted patterns. Skill to carve an appropriate pattern; whereas Will to stay consistent in performing that ritual.

Successful people develop habits, which failures do not like to. They develop the winning habits by utilizing their skills and by consistently forcing themselves in carving the pattern. Procrastination is one of the common human tendency; failures stick with this obvious tendency; whereas successful people

<u>practice a habit</u> of overcoming it by consistently pushing themselves to get the work done. Quitting in adverse conditions is another common approach of a human behavior. Failures do not like to put in that extra effort to stay in a race; as a result, they quit. Winners rejuvenate their 'Skills' and with their strong 'Will' put in that extra effort, even when it hurts. Successful people <u>practice a habit</u> of not quitting. We know that winners never quits and quitters never win.

This consistent application (Practice) of your improved **skills** with complete **will**; then become your habits and your habits then defines your destiny.

Remember, every thought we think is creating our future!

Connect your dots well to WIN.

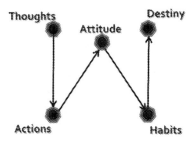

Prejudging

*O*ne *late evening, I was coming back from office. It was my day, as I was satisfied with my key achievements on that day. I was driving slowly with peace of mind, listening to melodious song; abruptly, a car overtook mine. This made me furious; I could not do anything other than scolding, cursing and charging the driver within. Anyway, I continued driving the same way enduring the uncontrollable instance. Few miles ahead, I found that the same car got thrashed in an accident. A crowd was gathered, ambulance splendid light infuriating the vision, people were murmuring over the incident. I thought, this had to happen with this kind of reckless driver. I stopped nearby and asked one of the persons gently; he informed that the driver got a heart attack. I was shocked and more than shock, I was frowned on my opinion (reckless driver) made about the driver without knowing the fact; I didn't even try to think on that line and swiftly formed an opinion.*

This is one of the inherent characteristics of human behavior. Knowingly or unknowingly, we tag people, thing and situation under different banners without even investigating the associated information or fiction. We are ready with tags in our mind; the moment we come across people, situation or things, we without vacillating, place a tag over it. We saw a black man, a tag is placed—poor, illiterate; on the contrary, a white skin may be tagged as rich or knowledgeable.

You glance at a person on the street and without your much of notice; your mind start creating some perceptions, based on that person's image captured by it. This ends up in tagging him or her with some labels of good or bad, appealing or dejecting, friendly or reserved, literate or illiterate, etc. You just happen to get in some situation and without much background and information, you start framing opinions on what you see. This is quite obvious with most of us, as an intrinsic & gravitated part of our behavior.

Some of our innate traits are helpful, while others may be disparaging. We need to identify the weary one and look into the ways to eliminate it. Practicing pragmatism is something required to overcome this deeply rooted behavior. We might not know; how adversely this innate behavior is affecting our lives and relationships.

Prejudging overtakes sanity. We decipher based on what we see, rather than what it is actually.

Prejudging may be painful for the victim. If you label someone as dejected based on look, you actually approach him or her in a same way. This affects the relationships; either the relationship will not groom or it may not even get planted, as your approach is now not naive, it is driven by the instruction of tag you placed; which of course may not be true. It can either way round as well; you tagged someone as a friend and made a move towards him accordingly. However, you may be deceived.

You can never create a strong platform for relationship with weak foundation of prejudging elements in it.

Saying NO

Mostly, we all believe that "NO" is a bitter pill to swallow. One is afraid of snapping NO to someone, who approached him with some request, task, help or order. No is treated like demon. Few may fear that by saying no, they may hurt the person's feeling and harm the relationship. But by saying "Yes" and stressing yourself to the level of breaking point is not a smart deal either. Saying yes at all occasion might win a game for you but certainly not the championship.

> To walk firm, you have to talk the right. Saying no at times is one of right way to walk firm.

To walk firm, you have to talk the right. Saying no at times is one of right way to walk firm.

Samuel was a sales executive in one of the MNC. He was very calm and cooperative person; he was always there to support his colleagues and contribute in whatever way he could to his organization. He was good in dealing with power point presentation. His colleagues admired him for his business acumen. Also he was enjoying a healthy relationship with his customers due to his promptitude.

It was his kids' school vacation, so Samuel decided to take them out for a week and have a whale of a time. But before, he could apply for leave, his boss declared his week off. He requested Samuel to postpone his plan till he come back. Samuel had no choice, other than to agree. His boss also requested him to prepare a presentation for him, which he was supposed to present in a management meeting. The management meeting was scheduled on the very next day of his boss arrival from his vacation.

As promised to his boss, soon Samuel started working on the presentation. An email popped up in between and buzzed the urgency. It was from his customer from another city, who ordered certain products but could not get delivered to him as per the commitment. He spent few hours in coordination and explored that the order was not executed due to delay in payment from the customer for his past invoices. The customer requested Samuel to collect the cheque from his office personally, as sending it by courier would take another 3-4 days and the order was urgent. So Samuel had to travel next morning for a day to his customer location so as to settle the issue.

Post his return from the tour; next day, after responding mails and getting through with the routine follow ups, he again found working on the presentation for his manager. This time, one of his colleagues with blurred face approached him for his help. Due to some emergency at home, his colleague had to take off for 2 days. He therefore asked for Samuel's help in following up with his customers, as some of the big orders are expected.

By now, his plate was already piled high with deadlines and obligations. Before he could look through his piled up plate, his cell buzzed. It was from his wife. With worried voice, she asked him to reach home urgently, as his kid required immediate attention of the doctor. A week passed with all these chaos around; neither, he could get through with the presentation, nor he could focus well on his routine follow ups. Further, he was not able to convert his colleague's sure shot prospect into business, as he could not address them timely.

Now, let's look at the after effects of the above scenario—

1. Finding the incomplete presentation on his joining back, his boss was furious. As a matter of showing his anger, he canceled Samuel's leave request.
2. Samuel's colleague blamed him for his slack in business, as according to him, Samuel may have intentionally not followed with his sure shot prospects. So he started criticizing Samuel.
3. Few Samuel's customers got annoyed and withdrawn the business, as they felt lack of

interest from Samuel due to no or delayed response to their business enquires.

4. Family got upset, as they were all set for the holiday trip and due to last minute cancellation, it scotched the snake.

What went wrong above with Samuel? Was he really incapable of handling multiple tasks? Was he really not effective in his approach?

The root cause analysis says that he was not able to say NO. There lied the problem. He was accepting everything coming on his way, without realizing how over burden he was already. May be he did not want to hurt his boss, his colleague and his customer who asked him to collect the cheque from his office instead of sending it by courier.

"NO" is considered as negative or rude response. In general, it is perceived that the one, who is wearing a hat with NO on it, is a person with negative mindset.

We believe that saying NO to certain task or activity is synonym to Inability, Not interested, Arrogance, Ignorance, non cooperation etc. That's the reason why most of us find it difficult to say no, when they really want to; worrying that it can reflect negative on their part. However, always and for everything nodding in yes can even be worst, as above.

In above case, the best possible way out could have been—

1. Samuel could have requested his boss to look for someone else this time to help him with this time by giving appropriate and correct reason.

2. He could have excused his customer from travelling to his location to collect the cheque by explaining his situation well. He should not have paid his time for his customer's ill organized payment schedule.

3. Before accepting his colleague's request, he should have scanned his priorities vis-à-vis time. His colleague could have understood and have approached someone else.

When you cram too many tasks into limited time span, you end up going out of shape. This will not just be frustrating for you, even for them who relied on you. It is not a good idea to bag a task just because you can't say No. If you can't justify the project you are going to man, it is advisable in favor of both the parties to say no to it and give clean bill of health.

Saying No is not an art. It is more of a requirement, as you have other fish to fry as well. If you keep on welcoming the task, which you can not accomplish, just because of your inability to refuse it; you will neither be fish, flesh, fowl nor good red herring. At the end, your condition would be like a fish in muddy water.

While saying no, you need to ascertain the following—

1. Assertiveness—You must have an assertive approach. Be positive when you do not want to take any further task onboard.
2. Give valid reason—Just saying no is not sufficient, you should attach valid reason to it.
3. Don't be guilty—You are not committing crime by saying no. You are just honest so do not carry a burden of guilt on your shoulder for this.
4. Be honest—Don't just fabricate the reason since you don't want to accept the task. Be honest with your take on not accepting the additional task. Honesty is something everyone expect and accept.
5. Be firm—Don't be shaky when saying no. Be firm but be polite.

There are benefits associated in saying NO. Let's have a look on those—

1. Your life will be balanced.
2. You can enjoy healthy relationships, as there will be no ambiguity
3. Mind will be in Peace.
4. Effectivity and Efficiency will be higher.

Saying No, is like grabbing a knife; grab it appropriately, else you will end up hurting yourself. You need to be affirmative while you practice refusing overloaded. But it is a great tool with grand benefits.

Decision Making

Confusion is about dealing with ambiguity and difficulty in making a decision to choose one out of the various available options. It is about listening to a reason and scoring a bull's eye. There has to be some rhyme or reason in making a decision.

One of my bosses was very good at decision making. He was so quick and accurate in this art that always brought me bolt from the blue. I used to wonder, whether it is a God's gift or a quality that can be learned. I tried to understand from him the secret of being so knack, but he himself never noticed the process behind it to explain it to me. But I truly wanted to be like him in decision making. Someone told me that if you have knowledge of the subject in which you are taking a decision, you will happen to be accurate and hasty. True, but again that was a broader aspect. Knowing something alone can't help you in selecting and making right calls. I wanted to get into the logical approach.

Almost, everyone come across the situations on day to day basis, wherein he/she gets stuck and find difficult to take an appropriate decision by selecting the right variable out of multiple opportunities.

Decisions should not be framed on the platform of snap judgement; it has to have the judicious selection and consideration of careful thoughts. Decision making is a fragment of our day to day activity. Necessity knows no laws, albeit an adoption of tested and proven approach will help to score the bull's eye.

Technically, there is a process in Decision Making. This process consists of 4 steps, viz.-

1. Identify Needs—Confusion arises only when a selection has to made from varied options to satisfy your needs. The very first step emphasis on identifying the specific needs, albeit the need may be more than one; but then priority has to be set.

2. Requirements to fulfil needs—Once the need is identified, then it is the step where it is mandatory to understand clearly, as to what are the requirements/processes that can help accomplishing those needs.

3. Sources—Third element of the process emphasis on the identification of the sources

which can help delivering the materials to achieve the end results.

4. <u>Actions</u>—Once need(s) has been identified, requirements/process has been understood and the sources to approach has been set, it is then the stage to set the frame of actions with clear and precise thoughts.

Once it is apparent—

1. What is needed;
2. Requirements thereof to accomplish the needs;
3. From where it can be delivered, and lastly;
4. How it can be achieved

Then, it would be less vulnerable to perplexing state of mind and the decision making would be much easier, efficient and effective.

Success is a child's play

"Success is not a child's play"; I am sure most of us have heard this very common statement. We must have heard it numerous times

from numerous sources. You wanted to go for trekking and your parents suggested that it is not a child's play; you shared your dream goal with your friends or colleagues and in turn you get snapped with the same statement. "It is not a child's play."

If you ask a man of wisdom, what are the secrets of success? Or, refer to books on secrets of success; you will be propounded with the endless list of the elements like hard work, determination, discipline, sincerity, dedication, perseverance etc. However, it is not so complicated. The theory of success is as simple as sticking stamps on the envelope.

At the end of this article, you will start believing that "**Success is indeed a child's play**."

Have you ever witnessed a toddler learning to walk?

He falls numerous times while struggling to stand on his own feet and take few steps forward. Interestingly, that does not affect his motivation at all. Why? Let's look at the reasons below—

1. He does not surrender. His focus is not on setbacks. His entire energy is working towards achieving the goal. How we adults react when we face a series of failure? We start creeping, blaming and slowly we start believing that it can't be done. Finally we surrender but a child doesn't.

2. No one is there to discourage him by telling that you can't do it. In our case, people are there to pull our legs, criticize us; but why? Children are innocents; as we grow, we lose this precious gift to jealousy, ego, selfishness and to an endless list of similar kind of ill emotions. As we all know the Law of Sowing and Reaping; if you treat the world innocently, the world in no way will consider you an enemy.

3. Even though if someone says to a child, "you can't do it", will he listen and incorporate it as his belief? He will not. It's not because he can't understand

NO, but because a child has his own belief. He is not driven by an external belief system. It is we adults, who takes the world as we find it, not the child. Child does not speak others' mind; it is we adult, who keep worrying about others' opinion and follow the set pattern of beliefs, not the child.

> It is not required to be serious in order to bag a success; sincerity is more than enough..

4. Child does not know what to blame, whom to and why to? He does not waste his energy in blaming; rather he demonstrates courage and takes another chance, yet another and another, till he achieves what he wants. What we do in failure? We start blaming, be it a family member, wife, boss, colleagues, friends, society, politicians, Government etc. Or if we do not find any one to blame, we will blame the situation and in worst case, we will not even hesitate to blame GOD.

5. When a child finally manages to take few steps, have you ever noticed the cheerfulness on the child's face? What does that reflect? It reflects celebration. He celebrates on his achievement open heartedly. For kids, success is not a fantasy; they find it in achieving what they want; be it a toy, spending time with parents, an elephant ride, watching cartoons, eating their favorite food

etc. When they achieve it, they celebrate it open heartedly.

When we were child, we all were engaged in certain kind of gaming activity—indoor or outdoor, right? Can you recall scoring a goal or hitting a century and then how you reacted? Loudly, cheerfully, crazily . . . . ! When was the last time, you celebrated with such an open heart? We adults keep on postponing the celebration for the next event. "I will celebrate when I will complete graduation", "I will celebrate when I will get a job", "I will celebrate when I get a promotion"; it then keep getting postponed to some other things and the transportation continues. We miss to understand that success is not followed by celebration; rather success is felt by celebration.

I would like to share a short little story of a father and a son. A father was walking down the street with his four years old son. Suddenly, it started raining; so he started stepping towards the nearby shed with one hand over his head and with the other hand, he was holding his son. The child's other arm was open to the sky; he was collecting few droplets of water in his tiny palm and was splashing that onto his face and drinking it in between.

That gives us a brilliant message here; when it rains, it rains evenly on all, no matter rich or poor, white or black, men or women, child or adult. We all are showered with the same level of energy and opportunities, but most of us have the arm over our own grief & belief and miss to receive the energy from nature. Like a child, few among us who received this energy and opportunity with open hands, swallowed it and felt it, are now known as Dhirubhai Ambani, Bill Gates, Michael Schumacher, Mohammed Ali, Sachin Tendulkar, Ronaldo and the list goes on.

It is not required to be serious in order to bag a success; sincerity is more than enough. What is required in addition is child like attitude—Be focused, be curious, maintain the innocence, don't keep space for blame, set your own belief and celebrate every achievement of yours without postponing it for the next event.

So next time, if someone says that the success is not the child's play, smile at him and say it is a child's play.

Thoughts to Destiny

It is scientifically proven that in a day, we encounter more than 60,000 thoughts in a day. A research suggests that out of this, 80% are

> Thoughts are like raw materials of a finished good. Change the quality of raw materials and the quality of finished product will be changed.

negative and frustrating. And it's only 20% which are energizing and motivating. We have to use an appropriate filter in order to keep negative thoughts away to settle down in our minds and stay motivated. Thoughts are like raw material of any finished goods. Change the quality of raw materials and the quality of finished products will be changed.

The kind of thoughts we allow to settle down in our mind after filtering, decides our attitude, which then demonstrated by the actions we incorporate and finally it decides our destiny.

We all must have heard that your thoughts can become your destiny. On the other hand, your desires can never be your destiny. Law of Attraction suggests, "You attract what you are and not what you want." Like in any journey; here too is a specific path from start point (thought) to finishing line (destiny). The key is to discover the right path. Many people starts well; with complete dedication and determination, they work hard to achieve their goals, but in spite of this, they fail to accomplish their goals. Why?

Let's understand this. A spark of thought is created, that encouraged to strive for a specific goal; so we put in hard work, dedication with complete determination to reach out to our target. Chances are there that we still might not get what we gunned for. Now, what happens is that once we face the failure, a thought has now got transmitted to an emotion, called worry. This negative emotion

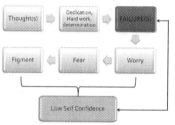

does not come alone; it comes with its sibling called fear. Both of these then generates figment in our mind. The figment then raises various doubts like—

1. Can I achieve my goal?
2. Am I capable of achieving that goal?
3. Is the goal realistic, is it possible?

These doubts then lower our self confidence. And we all know that with low self confidence, what we get in return is the failure. Again every time we face failure, it lowers our confidence. As a result, we quit. Now, there has to be a key to break this cycle between lower self confidence and failures. What is that key? That key is another thought! Thought in first stage inspired us to run and gun for the goal we targeted. Another kind of thought at this stage is required to spark motivation.

What kind of motivation this thought has to generate? Motivation to learn from mistakes after facing failure and a motivation to protect ourselves from getting trapped in twin sisters' cobweb—worry and fear. One thought will inspire you and another will motivate you to stay inspired. The picture then looks something like below—

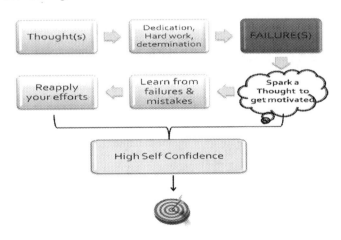

Our life is navigated by the thoughts we drive our minds. We do not have control over the external environment completely; but we always can monitor and tune our internal environment. Failures are not completely in our hand, what is in our control is to learn from the failures and mistakes; and reapply the efforts with full enthusiasm, as we did in the very first attempt. Most of the people quit the process, without knowing how close they where to their goal, when they quit. Quitting is not a negative term, but widely used in negative sense. Quitting can also be positive; quit your negative feelings, quit your fear and quit your worries, but don't quit your journey; a journey to success.

Visualization

I t is said that if you can visualize your goal, you can achieve it.

There is a misconception with many of the people on this; they said that even they visualized what they want, they could not achieve it. So for them, it was nothing more than the bookish thought. But does it really works? If it works, then why not all people is benefited from it?

There is no doubt that it works; but it works in its own way. What happen is, most of the people visualize, but they visualize results. Raheel wanted to become a rich and successful business tycoon in the textile industry in the country. He started visualizing himself as a rich businessman. But he could not even budge an inch to achieve it even after years of visualization. What went wrong there? He kept on visualizing an end results rather than the process. That's the key reason behind him not amount to anything. It may work, but chances are as little as a drop of water in a desert. He should have visualized the process like he is being heading a business meeting, forming a strategy, cracking a deal, winning the tender and contracts, etc. When we visualize the process, we activate our conscious mind; the signal is then been sent from conscious mind to all our organs to get synchronized with the imagination. This boosts our inner energy and raises the bar. When the energy level is raised, it has to flow. This flow of energy then gears up our thoughts, actions and activities in the same direction of visualization.

Visualizing helps aligning thoughts and actions. When our thoughts and actions work in the same direction, the ball has to roll.

Destiny and Distractions

Allí of us have some destiny to reach, by chance or by choice. Either way, our actions and attitude decides our path.

> We have some destiny to reach, by chance or by choice...

Destiny by chance, rarely happened and does not derived under the head of success; this gives a <u>feeling of surprise</u>. Whereas, when you choose your destiny, you decide your path and then you reach your goals, it is called Success! This gives a <u>feeling of achievement</u>.

On the way to destiny, you will always come across various distractions of different forms; which will off route you. It is therefore imperative that you should focus on your destiny and end goals only and do not get distracted by foreign thoughts.

Distraction works silently and doesn't get into the notice until major time pass away. It's therefore very dangerous. Now, the obvious thought is how to identify it before the situation takes your control.

Distractions are normally lead by negative emotions like anger, jealous, greed, laziness and so many other ill emotions. These tends to dilute the strength of yours and so as your confidence. When your flow of energy gets diluted, it readily flow downwards to a path, which doesn't have challenges to surmount. And when your life gets directed to a path with little or no challenge, you are on distracted path.

Where there is no challenge, there is no Success associated with it; there could only be surprises—good or bad.